DATE			

AFFECT AND CREATIVITY:
The Role of Affect and Play
in the Creative Process

PERSONALITY ASSESSMENT

A series of volumes edited by
Charles D. Spielberger and James N. Butcher

PIOTROWSKI • Dreams: A Key to Self-Knowledge
ARCHER • Using the MMPI with Adolescents
HARROWER/BOWERS • The Inside Story: Self-Evaluation Reflecting
Basic Rorschach Types
RUSS • Affect and Creativity: The Role of Affect in the Creative Process

AFFECT AND CREATIVITY:
The Role of Affect and Play in the Creative Process

Sandra Walker Russ

1993

LAWRENCE ERLBAUM ASSOCIATES, PUBLISHERS
Hillsdale, New Jersey   Hove and London

Lawrence Erlbaum Associates, Inc., Publishers
365 Broadway
Hillsdale, New Jersey 07642

Library of Congress Cataloging in Publication Data

Russ, Sandra Walker
   Affect and Creativity : the role of affect and play in the
creative process / Sandra Walker Russ.
      p.   cm. — (Personality assessment)
   Includes bibliographical references and index.
   ISBN 0-8058-0986-4
   1. Creative Ability.   2. Affect (Psychology)   3. Emotions and
cognition.   4. Personality and Cognition.   I. Title.   II. Series.
BF408.R79   1993
153.3'5 — dc20   92-22163
                                                                 CIP

Books published by Lawrence Erlbaum Associates are printed
on acid-free paper, and their bindings are chosen for strength
and durability.

Printed in the United States of America
10 9 8 7 6 5 4 3 2 1

To my parents
      Edith and Wilson Walker
   for an honest and loving start
And to my husband
      Tom Brugger
         for an honest and loving
       present.

Contents

Preface   ix

Chapter One
Affect and Creativity   1

Chapter Two
Primary Process, Affect, and Creativity   17

Chapter Three
Children's Fantasy, Play, Affective Expression, and Creativity   32

Chapter Four
The Affect in Play Scale   43

Chapter Five
Personality Trait Approach to Creativity   60

Chapter Six
Mood-Induction and Motivational Systems
Approaches to Creativity   71

Chapter Seven
    Neurological Processes, Artificial Intelligence, and Creativity   **79**

Chapter Eight
    Implications for Home, Educational,
    and Therapeutic Environments   **88**

Chapter Nine
    Affective Components of the Creative Process:
    Conclusions and Future Research Directions   **100**

Appendix: The Affect in Play Scale   **110**

References   **119**

Author Index   **130**

Subject Index   **134**

Preface

Creativity is an exciting process. To observe it, recognize it, or experience it are some of the most satisfying aspects of the human condition. One of the dangers of studying or analyzing the creative process is that it can become pedestrian. Indeed, one of the current debates in the field is whether or not creativity is simply an example of logical problem solving or involves other kinds of processes. The main benefit of studying creativity is that we will come to understand the processes involved and will be able to enhance the development of creativity in future generations.

What do we know about creativity? We know a good deal about what creativity is — especially about the cognitive components. We are just beginning to learn about the affective components of the creative process. Although psychoanalytic theory has discussed the importance of affect in creativity, the field has just begun to empirically investigate the specific affective processes and mechanisms involved in creativity and to search for a comprehensive theoretical understanding. The major questions addressed in this book are: (a) Is affect an important part of the creative process? and (b) If so, how is affect involved in creative thinking? We learn about the role of affect in creativity from three major sources. First, descriptions of the creative process by creative individuals can give clues as to how affect comes into the picture. Second, research on cognitive-affective processes and affect in cognition is beginning to shed some light on how these processes interact. Personality trait research and creativity is an important related area, as is research on children's play. Third, theoretical frameworks that integrate and encompass observations and empirical findings suggest future studies that move the field ahead.

Why is it important to learn about the role of affect in creativity? In general, investigating the interaction between cognitive and affective processes involved in divergent thinking, memory, and cognitive flexibility will give us a fuller picture of the processes involved in the creative act. To study only the cognitive processes involved in creativity misses half of the picture. Emotional development has not been emphasized as much as cognitive development in our educational institutions. As we learn how cognitive and affective processes are intertwined, there will be implications for educational reform and for childrearing practices. One of the major problems in studying the role of affect in creativity has been the lack of adequate measures of affective processes. As new measures and experimental paradigms are developed (or rediscovered), the necessary research is able to be carried out.

The purpose of this book is to synthesize the information that exists about affect and creativity and to suggest a theoretical model that will encompass what we currently know. The information that currently exists is from rather disparate literatures and theoretical approaches. If we can identify some common findings and themes in a variety of descriptions and research studies, we can better determine whether and how affect is involved in creative thinking and have a road map for future research directions. Because my own theoretical orientation is psychodynamic and my research program has been with children, this book contains a somewhat greater coverage of the child literature from a psychodynamic–developmental perspective than of other populations and theoretical approaches. Historically, psychodynamic theory has had much to say about affect and creativity. This volume attempts to integrate the classic psychoanalytic approach to creativity with other theoretical approaches in social and cognitive psychology and with the empirical literature.

Throughout all of the chapters, there is a focus on the role of affect in creativity. Chapter 1 discusses definitions of creativity, aspects of the creative process, and major theoretical approaches to creativity. It presents a general model of affect and creativity, which is discussed in detail throughout the book. This model spells out the connections among affective and cognitive processes important to the creative process. Chapter 2 reviews in depth psychoanalytic theory, primary process thinking, and research in this area. Chapters 3 and 4 review major empirical work in the child area. Chapter 3 reviews the research on children's play and creative problem solving as well as relevant studies in the play therapy literature. The play therapy literature is especially important because it addresses the question of how affect influences cognitive processes. Chapter 4 presents a new scale for measuring affect in children's play, the Affect in Play Scale, which my students at Case Western Reserve University and I developed and researched. Reliability and validity of the scale are reviewed. The relationships among children's play, creativity, and coping ability are also reviewed. Chapter 5 discusses personality correlates of creativity in children and adults. The personality trait studies are interpreted with a specific focus on implications for the role of affect in creativity. Recent work on adjustment and creativity is also reviewed in this chapter. Chapter 6 discusses other major research programs in the area of creativity that speak to the role of affect, such as Amabile's work on motivation and creativity and Isen's work on mood induction. Chapter 7 reviews work on artificial intelligence and computer modeling relevant to affect and creativity. In addition, neurological processes as they relate to affect and cognition are discussed. Chapter 8 presents implications for childrearing practices, classroom experiences, and psychotherapy. Chapter 9 summarizes the major points in the book, gives the major conclusions that evolve from the research, and offers suggestions for future work.

ACKNOWLEDGMENTS

I wish to express my appreciation to a number of individuals who contributed, in various ways, to the development of my research and of this book. First, I am deeply grateful to Irv Weiner for his belief in my work and his willingness to take a chance on me and give me a start in academia; to Charles Spielberger, who first proposed the idea of writing a book that integrated my work in the area of creativity; and to Douglas Schultz, for his constant encouragement and statistical consultation over the years. I also wish to thank Provost Richard Zdanis for his flexibility and support of my work on the project while I was in the provost's office. And I am appreciative of the support of the faculty of the Psychology Department at Case Western Reserve University.

My graduate students have been inspirational and have contributed greatly to the evolving of my ideas and research program. Special thanks to Jim Murray, Anna Grossman-McKee, Mark Kleinman, Nancy Peterson, Hilary Einhorn Katz, and Beth Christiano for their work in the area of creativity and children's play.

I am grateful to Our Lady of Good Counsel Elementary School, Cleveland Heights and Shaker Heights school districts, and St. Ann's Parish for permitting the research studies to be carried out in their schools. I am especially appreciative of the support of Sister Mary Ann Mozser for enabling a longitudinal research project to be carried out.

Thank you also to Wendy Williams, whose typing of the manuscript and investment in the project was an essential ingredient for which I am grateful.

The excellent work of Hollis Heimbouch and the editorial staff at Lawrence Erlbaum Associates is greatly appreciated.

Finally, I wish to thank my husband, Tom, for providing the support for me to do the work I needed to do.

Sandra W. Russ

1 Affect and Creativity

The study of creativity is the study of some of the most valued processes in human development. To study creativity is to focus on what is optimal in the individual. Because of the rather magnetic quality of the creativity area, the topic of creativity has attracted a large number of researchers and scholars from a variety of disciplines and theoretical perspectives.

This chapter reviews definitions of creativity; stages of creativity; cognitive, affective, and personality processes important in creativity; and presents a new model of affect and creativity. This model is discussed in detail throughout the book.

A first task for the field has been that of definition. What is creativity? There seems to be a consensus in the field about what makes something creative.

THE CREATIVE PRODUCT

A useful distinction is that of the creative product as opposed to the creative process (Golann, 1963; MacKinnon, 1962). The creative product is the output of the individual. It is the output that is to be judged as creative or not creative. Of the numerous attempts to identify the criteria by which to judge a product as creative, two characteristics are repeatedly listed (Hayes, 1978; MacKinnon, 1962). For a product to be judged as creative, it must be: (a) unique, original, novel; (b) good, that is, adaptive, useful, aesthetically pleasing, according to the standards of the particular discipline.

Both components are necessary. There must be a newness to the

1

theoretical solution or artistic piece. Torrance (1988), in a review of definitions of creativity, concluded that newness is a major criterion of judging the creative product. A product is creative if old facts are integrated in new ways, new relationships emerge from old ideas, or there is a new configuration. Novelty, however, is not a sufficient criteria. It is also necessary that the product be good (i.e., aesthetically appealing if it is a work of art; an accurate solution to a scientific problem; a useful invention for consumers). Vernon (1989) put forth a comprehensive definition of creativity that includes these major components, "Creativity means a person's capacity to produce new or original ideas, insights, restructuring, inventions, or artistic objects, which are accepted by experts as being of scientific, aesthetic, social, or technological value" (p. 94). Thus, cultural values and norms are an inevitable part of the criteria for judging something to be creative. That is, of course, a problem when a work is good, but ahead of its time and goes unrecognized as being creative for a number of decades. Occasionally, these two criteria conflict. Something might be so new that it breaks the rules of the discipline by which something is judged to be good, and time is needed for the standards to catch up with the advance in the field. One way around this occasional lack of recognition might be to judge whether or not the work is original and has some potential for being judged as good. If so, final judgment about its creativity could be held in abeyance. The work or solution could be placed on a potentially creative list. This list could be used by researchers in the area of creativity. The "cold fusion" experiments, the paintings of Andy Warhol, and the music of Philip Glass might be candidates for this potentially creative list. This list could be used by researchers in the area of creativity.

Given these two criteria for a product to be judged as creative, the question is often asked, "can children be truly creative?" Although they can generate new and good products, the products are usually not at a level of sophistication necessary to truly contribute to an area. However, if one considers whether or not a product is new and good for that age group, then children can be considered as generators of creative products. If age norms are taken into consideration, then it makes sense to talk about children being creative and to study their creative processes. A point made by Thurstone (1952) seems relevant here. Thurstone stated that even though a discovery may have already occurred, if it is new to the thinker, then it is a creative act. Thus, children could demonstrate a number of creative acts that would involve creative processes.

A major question in studying creativity is "what are the processes that are part of the creative act?" What cognitive and affective processes are involved in the creative process and increase the likelihood that an individual will generate a creative product? If we can identify the different processes involved and the nature of their interaction, then we can begin to develop a picture of the nature of the creative act.

STAGES OF CREATIVITY

The first well-known attempt to conceptualize the creative process was by Wallas in 1926. Although Wallas did not identify specific processes, he did articulate different stages that reflect different processes. Although Wallas' stages are crude and global, his four-stage model has helped order our thinking about the creative process. A detailed discussion of this model can be found in Armbruster (1989). His four-stage model consists of:

1. Preparation Stage—information gathering, mastering the knowledge base, identifying the problem. It is in this stage that the basic techniques and knowledge base of a particular domain are mastered. For example, techniques of painting are mastered or the research literature is totally investigated. It is probably in this stage that basic intellectual processes are important in determining the rapidity of learning and the complexity of issues that are tackled.

2. Incubation Stage—ideas incubate without the individual directly, logically working on the problem. It is in this stage that processes unique to the creative process are so important. It is also in this stage that Wallas and others (Armbruster, 1989; Sinnott, 1970) introduced the concept of the unconscious. Problems are not consciously worked on, but much restructuring and free associating occurs outside of conscious awareness. In chapter 2, there are several descriptions by creative individuals of the subjective experience of the incubation stage. Thoughts are permitted to roam in a free-ranging manner. It is here that affective processes may play an especially important role.

3. Illumination Stage—the solution to the problem occurs or is recognized. The artistic plan develops. This stage is often referred to as the "aha" experience of the creative scientist. In reality, as many have pointed out (Gruber & Davis, 1988, Weisberg, 1988), reaching a solution is probably a gradual process in most instances. The sudden illumination occurrence is probably the least frequent manner by which a solution occurs.

4. Verification Stage—the solution must now be evaluated. Is it indeed good? The hypothesis must be tested; the painter must stand back and evaluate and rework the painting. Critical thinking and logical thinking must be dominant in this stage.

In general, the basic cognitive processes of logic, memory, and abstract thinking should be dominant in the first and last stages. Different types of cognitive processes should be dominant in Stages 2 and 3. Stages 2 and 3 are especially important in creative problem solving and creative artistic expression. It is in the incubation stage that affective processes most likely play a major role.

As Gruber (1989) correctly pointed out, Wallas' stage model is incomplete. It does not include the early stage of problem finding (Arlin, 1986; Getzels & Csikszentmihalyi, 1976) or the final stage of expansive application of the creative product. However, Wallas' basic stages remain theoretically useful and continue to be the basis for training approaches (Torrance, 1988).

As Vinacke (1952) stressed, the stages of this creative process are probably not so ordered as Wallas first proposed. Individuals go back and forth rapidly between the stages, sometimes letting their thoughts roam, sometimes calling on their critical thinking faculties. It is the ability to shift between stages that is important to the creative process, perhaps involving the ability to gain access to or call into play creative cognitive and affective processes (or let them occur). Psychoanalytic theorists refer to this ability as "regression in the service of the ego" (Kris, 1952).

COGNITIVE CREATIVE PROCESSES

A key theoretical question in the area of creativity is "what cognitive and affective processes are involved in the creative process?" Much of the focus in the area of creativity research has been on cognitive processes.

Guilford (1950, 1967, 1968) made major theoretical contributions to the area of creativity in that he identified and investigated cognitive processes not previously focused on in tests of intelligence. In general, Guilford believed that creativity was made up of many different components. He discussed both cognitive processes and personality traits as contributing to creativity. His research, however, focused on cognitive processes. Guilford's work was based on several principles that continue to be the basis for creativity research today.

The first principle was that creative abilities fall on a continuum. Guilford (1968) did not hold to the view that only a select number of eminent individuals were creative and should be studied. All individuals possess creative abilities to some degree, "creative acts can therefore be expected, no matter how frequent or how infrequent, of almost all individuals" (p.82). Thus, creativity can be studied in normal populations.

A second principle was that creative thinking is something different from what intelligence tests measure. Intelligence tests measure logical thought processes that reflect convergent thinking. There is one best answer for a problem, not a variety of responses as in creative divergent thinking.

Research has supported the concept that creative abilities are separate abilities from what we define as intelligence (Kogan, 1983). Most studies find low to moderate positive correlations between creativity tests and intelligence tests (Runco, 1991). Until recently, it was widely accepted that a certain amount of intellectual ability was necessary for creativity to occur. Studies show that in the upper ranges of intelligence, the correlation with creativity is zero (Kogan, 1983). This has been known as the threshold theory. However, work by Runco (1991) suggested that the relationship between creativity and intelligence is a function of the measures used and the samples studied. He concluded that the threshold theory is "at least partly a psychometric artifact" (p. 171).

Guilford's third principle is that creativity is really a form of problem solving — not a magical, mysterious process. Guilford also stated that Wallas' four-stage model of creativity is consistent with other models of problem solving.

Guilford (1968) identified cognitive processes that were unique to creativity. He concluded that two major categories of cognitive processes were important in the creative process. First, divergent production abilities were uniquely important in the creative process. Guilford thought that the key concept underlying divergent production abilities is variety. One can generate a variety of solutions to a problem or associations to a word. Divergent thinking is thinking that goes off in different directions. For example, a typical item on a divergent thinking test would be "how many uses for a brick can you think of?" As Guilford (1968) stated "divergent thinking is a matter of scanning one's stored information to find answers to satisfy a special search model" (p. 105). A broad base of search and free-ranging scanning ability increases divergent thinking production. Wallach (1970) stated that divergent thinking is dependent on the flow of ideas and the "fluidity in generating cognitive units" (p. 1240). He stressed the importance of the ability to "ride the associative currents." Divergent thinking should be especially important in the incubation stage of Wallas' stages of creativity. Divergent thinking is discussed in detail throughout this book.

The second category of abilities relevant to creative ability is what Guilford termed *transformation* abilities. These abilities enable the individual to transform or revise what one knows into new patterns or configurations. A flexibility to reorganize and break out of old sets is important here. The individual reorders, redefines, or reinterprets what is currently known. One sees a new solution to a problem that is different from the usual approach. Much of Guilford's research focuses on identifying cognitive processes that make up these two categories of abilities — divergent thinking and transformation abilities and devising tests of these abilities.

Guilford conceptualized these abilities as cognitive abilities. Although he felt that personality characteristics were important to creativity, he believed that they were separate from these cognitive processes. However, as we see later, recent research suggests that affective processes influence divergent thinking abilities and transformation abilities.

Currently, major work on the cognitive processes involved in creativity has been carried out by a number of researchers (Langley & Jones, 1988; Simon, 1977; Sternberg, 1988; Weisberg, 1986, 1988). Sternberg (1988; Sternberg & Davidson, 1982) stressed the importance of insight in creative thought. Sternberg and Davidson (1982) postulated that three types of insights are involved in creativity. Selective encoding involves separating relevant from irrelevant information. Selective combination entails synthesizing isolated pieces of information into unified wholes. Information is organized in new ways. Selective comparison involves relating new information to old information. These three types of knowledge acquisition set the stage for creative insights. One might speculate that divergent thinking abilities and transformation abilities partially underlie these types of knowledge acquisition and insight abilities.

Weisberg (1986, 1988) viewed creativity as another form of problem solving that involves matching what one knows with the situation. He stressed the incremental nature of problem solving. There are few real leaps of insight. Rather, novel products evolve in small steps that utilize local memory searches. The incremental nature of problem solving is true in both science and art. Weisberg would agree with Guilford that creative thinking does not involve extraordinary abilities, but rather ordinary cognitive processes that are found in all individuals.

On the other hand, Metcalfe (1986) presented evidence that some insight problems are different from memory retrieval tasks. She used a "feeling of knowing" paradigm to determine whether similar processes were involved in an insight problem and a memory based trivia problem. In two studies, she found that people could predict memory performance fairly well, but could not predict performance for insight problems. She concluded that insight problems do involve a sudden illumination that can not be predicted in advance.

Simon (1977) greatly influenced the field with his work on models of information processing and problem solving as they apply to creativity. He also led the way in the area of computer simulation of creative problem solving. His work on selective forgetting and familiarization in memory helps explain the insight process. Langley and Jones (1988) developed a computational model of scientific insight. They stressed the importance of use of analogy in creative problem solving. Insight involves the recognition, evaluation, and elaboration of analogies. Memory processes are important in recognizing appropriate analogies for new situations. The role of computer simulation in the study of creativity is discussed in chapter 7.

AFFECT AND CREATIVITY

The term *affect* is used throughout this book, rather than *emotion,* because affect seems to be the more inclusive concept. I agree with Auke Tellegen who recently (1989) stated that emotion is really a subset of affect. He referred to a rather simple definition of affect in the American Heritage Dictionary as a feeling or emotion as distinct from cognition. Emotion is defined as a state of aroused feeling or agitation. Tellegen's articulation is consistent with Izard's (1977) view of affect as a broad set of events that includes emotions and drives. It is also consistent with Moore and Isen's (1990) conceptualization of affect as feeling states that are pervasive and nonspecific affective events. Emotions are more "interrupting types of experiences that are typically more focal in terms of both target and behavioral response than are feeling states" (p. 2).

It was the cognitive style theorists and psychoanalytic theorists, sometimes combined in the same individual, who first began to think about the influence of affect on cognition, such as affect on divergent thinking. Work in the 1960s began to investigate the cognitive style area. As Kogan (1976) pointed out, the cognitive style construct reflects an interface between cognition and personality. Cognitive style encompassed such concepts as field-dependence-independence (autonomy from the stimulus field), reflection-impulsivity (amount of reflection in problem solving), and style of categorization (breadth vs. narrowness). Individual differences in these kinds of cognitive processes were associated with personality components. The research on cognitive style variables was important because it attempted to measure constructs that reflected both cognitive and personality components.

As Kogan (1983) stated, active research programs on cognitive styles from a psychoanalytic perspective have not continued. However, the work of Gardner and Moriarity (1968) and of Klein (1970) from the Menninger Foundation group helped to lay a theoretical framework that pointed to the importance of the interaction between cognition and personality processes.

Current research programs conceptualize in terms of cognitive-affective interaction (Amabile, 1983; Isen, Daubman, & Nowicki, 1987, 1990; Russ, 1987). Current creativity researchers and theoreticians are recognizing the importance of affect in the creative process (Csikszentmihalyi, 1990a; Runco, in press; Shaw, in press). Previous research programs in the cognitive style area and in the personality and creativity area had been the major areas of investigation of cognitive–affective interaction during the last 30 years. Zimiles (1981) correctly pointed out that, too often, the measures utilized in research studies have been brief and have not reflected the complexity of the original constructs. I would add that there is a need for specific measures of affective processes. The research on creativity and personality traits is an important area and may offer clues to specific affective processes involved in creativity (see chapter 5). The wealth of literature in this area shows a pattern of personality traits that are related to creativity in children and adults. Future research should be more focused on specific affective and cognitive processes in order to move the field ahead and identify the nature of cognitive–affective relationships.

A MODEL OF AFFECT AND CREATIVITY

What follows is a model of affective processes, personality traits, and cognitive abilities that are important to the creative process (see Figs. 1.1 and 1.2). This model is an attempt to spell out the connections among affective and cognitive processes important to the creative process. There is a need in the field for a comprehensive model of affect, personality, and creative cognitive abilities. Although the literature speaks to relationships between affect and cognition in specific areas, there has been no attempt to pull it all together. This model is my current conceptualization of a comprehensive model based on the research and clinical literature.

In this model of affect and creativity, the major cognitive abilities that emerge as unique to and important in the creative process are linked to related specific affective processes and to global personality traits. In some cases the personality traits are behavioral reflections of the underlying affective process. One assumption of this model is that these specific affective processes and personality traits facilitate creative cognitive abilities. Reciprocal interactions probably occur, as well.

Figure 1.1 presents the cognitive and affective processes. The links between the processes are based on theory and the empirical literature. Although we may eventually discover that all of these processes are interrelated, at the moment some relationships appear to be dominant. Figure 1.2 adds the personality traits to the model. For cognitive and affective categories, each box identifies a separate process. For personality traits, several different traits are included in each box, depending on which traits tend to be related to specific affective and cognitive processes.

I present, at this point, a brief overview of the model, without going into individual areas in depth. An in-depth discussion and literature review in each area occurs in relevant chapters throughout the book.

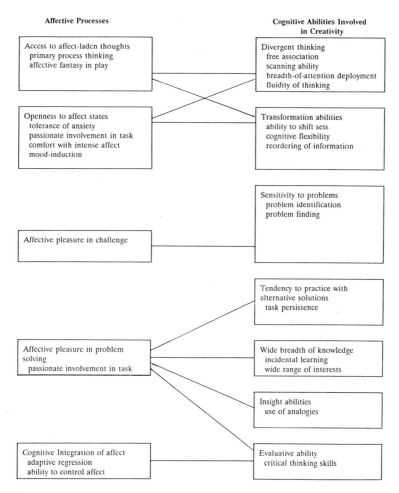

FIG. 1.1. Affect and creativity, a model.
  A major assumption of this model is that these specific affective processes facilitate creative cognitive processes. It is probable that reciprocal interaction occurs.

Cognitive Abilities

As previously discussed, there is some consensus in the literature about what cognitive abilities are involved in the creative process. The list presented here is a distillation of the major cognitive components thought to be involved in the creative act.

Guilford's two categories of cognitive processes are at the top of the list. *Divergent thinking* is one major cognitive ability that encompasses such concepts as free association, broad scanning ability, and fluidity of

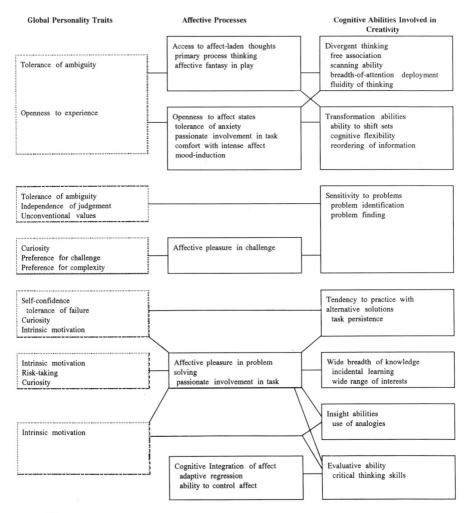

FIG. 1.2. Affect and creativity, a model.
In this model of affect and creativity, the major cognitive abilities that emerge as unique to and imortant in the creative process are linked to related specific affective processes and to global personality traits. In some cases, the personality traits are behavioral reflections of the underlying affective process. One assumption of this model is that these specific affective processes and personality traits facilitate creative cognitive abilities.

thinking. The second cognitive category is *transformation abilities,* which is reflected in the ability to shift sets, to think flexibly, to utilize different problem-solving approaches, and to reorder information. This concept has also been referred to as a cognitive flexibility–cognitive rigidity dimension in the cognitive style literature.

Guilford (1950) and others (Getzels & Csikszentmihalyi, 1976) identified *sensitivity to problems* and *problem finding* as an important cognitive ability in the creative individual. One must be able to identify the problem to be solved, which others may have missed, before tackling the problem.

The ability to try *alternative problem-solving* approaches is another important cognitive ability. Although this may be related to Guilford's transformation ability (the ability to shift sets and perceive alternative solutions), there may also be a more cognitive–behavioral ability that involves practice in applying different models. Task persistence and engaging in trial and error behavior is often mentioned as important in creative problem solving (Weisberg, 1988).

Breadth of knowledge and wide range of interests has also been frequently cited in lists of creative cognitive abilities (Barron & Harrington, 1981). A wide range of facts, information, analogies, and experiences provides much to draw on when attempting to develop a novel solution or configuration.

Sternberg's (1988) concept of different types of *insight* and synthesizing abilities are especially important in creative problem solving. These knowledge acquisition skills involve different types of synthesis and insight important in creative thinking.

Although not unique to creative thinking, critical thinking and *evaluative ability* are essential to the creative act (Guilford, 1950; Runco, 1991). It is crucial in Wallas' verification stage that the solution to the problem, the painting, or the product is judged to be good. The individual must stand back and evaluate the ideas, association, or composition and refine it. Without critical thinking ability, the other cognitive abilities are like unavailable resources. They may be present, but they cannot work for the individual or for the creative process.

Personality Traits

There is also a consensus in the literature about which personality traits are found in creative individuals or relate to tests of creativity. Major research programs in the area of personality and creativity (Barron, 1969; Gough, 1979; MacKinnon, 1965; McCrae & Costa, 1987; Roe, 1972) led to a personality profile of the creative individual. Figure 1.2 lists the major global categories of personality traits that emerge in the research literature. This list of traits is consistent with the conclusions of Barron & Harrington (1981) in their recent thorough review of the personality and creativity literature. The research base is mainly with adults, but the research with children paints a consistent profile. Some gender differences do emerge. In chapter 5 I discuss the findings of the personality trait research in detail.

The major personality traits important in the creative process are:

- tolerance of ambiguity;
- openness to experience;
- possessing unconventional values;
- independence of judgement;
- curiosity;
- preference for challenge and complexity;
- self-confidence;
- propensity for risk-taking;
- and intrinsic motivation.

AFFECTIVE PROCESSES

Recently, over the last 10 years, research programs have begun to look at specific affective processes that are related to or facilitate cognitive processes. This model is the first attempt to systematically identify specific affective processes involved in creativity. There has been enough work done so that we can begin to see a pattern. Important research questions are: Which specific affective processes are related to which cognitive processes?; What is the nature of the relationship?; Do these affective processes facilitate these cognitive abilities?; Do the cognitive abilities influence the affective processes?; If so, what are the mechanisms?

Five affective processes emerge as important in creativity. The five affective processes listed in Figs. 1.1 and 1.2 are broad categories. The model links the affective processes to personality traits as well as to the cognitive abilities. Some of the personality traits are reflections of these underlying affective processes, at least to some degree. Other personality traits are probably not related to specific affective processes.

Two broad affective processes related to creative cognitive abilities are access to affect-laden thoughts and openness to affect states.

- *Access to affect-laden thoughts* is the ability to call up cognitive material with affect-laden content. Primary process thinking and affective fantasy in daydreams and in play are examples of this kind of ability. Thoughts involving affect themes such as aggressive and sexual ideation illustrate this kind of blending of affect and cognition.
- *Openness to affect states* is the ability to experience the affect itself. Comfort with intense affect, the ability to experience and tolerate anxiety, and passionate involvement in a task or issue are examples of openness to affect states.

Two other more specific affective processes that can be identified as important to creativity are affective pleasure in challenge and affective pleasure in problem solving.

- *Affective pleasure in challenge* involves the excitement and tension involved in identifying the problem and working on the task.
- *Affective pleasure in problem solving* is the deep pleasure and passion involved in solving the problem, achieving insight, or completing a musical composition that sounds exactly right.

Finally, the overall cognitive control of the affective process is important.

- *Cognitive integration and modulation of affective material* is a cognitive–affective process crucial in adaptive creative functioning. Although this category is probably more cognitive than affective, it warrants inclusion because it reflects both cognition and affect, and it is so important in the creative process.

Relationships Among Cognitive Processes, Affective Processes, and Personality Traits

The research literature and theory suggest that the most important affective processes involved in creativity are those that relate to the very pure cognitive abilities, like divergent thinking and the ability to shift sets, that are unique to the creative process. Therefore, access to affect-laden thoughts and openness to affect states would be of major importance. Indeed, the bulk of the research evidence links these processes to creativity. The specific mechanisms need to be spelled out, but the assumption here is that affect influences cognition. Certainly, there are neurological underpinnings to these relationships. Possible models are discussed in chapter 7.

Some of the other cognitive abilities important to creativity, like wide breadth of knowledge, persistence in task, and sensitivity to problems are really a combination of cognitive abilities and behavioral tendencies. Therefore, some global personality traits are more important here. Certain personality traits influence behaviors that increase the likelihood that a creative act will occur. Affective processes of pleasure in challenge and problem solving would also play a role.

At this point, I review the proposed relationships very briefly. Only a few of the relevant research studies are referenced in this section. Detailed reviews of the literature come in later chapters. As the relationships are discussed here, we focus on the list of cognitive processes presented in Fig. 1.2 and take them in order.

Looking first at divergent thinking and transformation abilities, those cognitive processes relatively unique to creative thinking, the most substan tiated relationships in the research literature are those between access to affect-laden thoughts and divergent thinking, (Dudek & Verreault, 1989; Pine & Holt, 1960; Russ, 1988b), access to affect-laden thoughts and transformation abilities (Russ, 1982), openness to affect states and divergent thinking (Isen et al., 1987; Lieberman, 1977; Russ & Grossman-McKee, 1990) and openness to affect states and transformation abilities (Isen et al., 1987). In essence, children and adults who have access to affect-laden thoughts and fantasy are more creative than individuals who are less able to access this material. Children who are able to express and experience affect in play are more creative than children who are less able. Also, Isen's (Isen et al., 1987) mood-induction work shows that induced positive affect states facilitate creative thinking in adults. Research also shows, and theory suggests, that access to affect-laden material and openness to internal affect states relates to personality traits of tolerance of ambiguity and openness to experience (McCrae & Costa, in press). These personality traits also relate to divergent thinking (McCrae & Costa, 1987) and transformation abilities. Thus, two of the key affective processes identified in the creative process also relate to some of the key personality traits associated with creativity. Probably, only a small portion of the variance in the personality traits is accounted for by these affective processes. It makes sense that tolerance of ambiguity and openness to experience would be related to the cognitive abilities of divergent thinking and transformation abilities. To really have a free flow of associations, one must be comfortable with logical contradictions and the tension that develops when conflicting ideas are thought about simultaneously.

Looking now at the sensitivity to cognitive ability, the personality traits of tolerance of ambiguity, independence of judgment, and unconventional values would be important in helping an individual to "see" the problem, where others have not. Perceptual defenses would not need to be called on to "not see" the inherent problem and keep the individual comfortable. Curiosity and preference for challenge and complexity would also play a role here, as would the affective pleasure involved in seeing the problem and beginning to tackle it. Voss and Means (1989) discussed the attraction of the challenge once the problem is identified for the creative individual. They discussed the negative affect involved in seeing the problem and implied that the anticipation of the positive affect involved in solving the problem is a motivating force. However, it is possible that the tension involved in seeing the problem is not all negative. Like the affective pleasure in mounting the first hill on a roller coaster, the tension has its negative and positive aspects. Runco (in press) discussed the importance of tension in facilitating creative effort.

Self-confidence is probably most important in helping the individual to persist in the task, try alternative solutions, and tolerate repeated failure before a novel and good solution occurs. Curiosity and intrinsic motivation also play a role in keeping the individual on task. Anticipation of affective pleasure in finding the solution is important in encouraging task persistence. Passionate involvement in the task has often been noted as characteristic of creative individuals (Anastasi & Schaeffer, 1969).

Intrinsic motivation, risk-taking behavior, and curiosity would all increase the likelihood that an individual would engage in behaviors and have experiences that would increase their knowledge base. Affective pleasure in the task would also be important here. Thus, individuals would accumulate a wide breadth of knowledge that they could call on in their creative endeavors.

Looking now at insight abilities, taking affective pleasure in problem solving would be an important reinforcer when the "aha" experience occurred. The pleasure taken when the problem is solved or the painting is just right is probably an important affective component of the insight process. Amabile (1983) stressed the importance of the affective nature of the reward in problem solving. In addition, positive affect would help the individual recognize the correct solution when the right combination occurs. Metcalfe's (1986) work showed that people's subjective feeling in insight problems is that they suddenly know the solution. There is some evidence that access to affect-laden thoughts and access to affect states may facilitate the insight process (Jausovec, 1989). This cognitive–affect link remains largely unexplored.

Finally, affective pleasure in the task would be important in motivating the individual to do the work necessary to evaluate the product. Intrinsic motivation is an important trait in this process as well. The global capacity to cognitively control and integrate the affective material would be important in enabling evaluative ability, critical thinking, and logical thought processes to become dominant at appropriate times.

This model of affect and creativity is sketchy and is presented as an initial road map to help us think about affect and creativity and to guide us in future research directions. Empirical links need to be strengthened, other affective processes identified, and cause and effect demonstrated where it exists. In addition, more research needs to be carried out investigating the interrelationships among the cognitive variables, as well as among the personality and affect variables.

One can also apply this model to Wallas' stage theory and speculate as to which cognitive, personality, and affective processes are important in different stages of creativity (see Fig. 1.3). The major affective processes important in creativity would occur during the incubation stage, when divergent thinking and transformation abilities are so important. Affective pleasure in challenge would be important in the preparation stage (and perhaps anticipated affective pleasure in problem solving); access to

Wallas' Stages	Cognitive Abilities	Affective Processes	Personality Traits
Preparation	Sensitivity to problems Wide breadth of knowledge master knowledge base	Affective pleasure in challenge	Curiosity Tolerance of ambiguity Risk taking Intrinsic motivation Preference for challenge and complexity
Incubation	Divergent thinking Transformation abilities Tendency to practice with alternative solutions	Access to affect-laden thoughts primary process Openness to affect states	Openness to experience Tolerance of ambiguity Self-confidence Preference for challenge
Illumination	Evaluative ability Insight abilities	Access to affect-laden thoughts Openness to affect states Affective pleasure in problem solving	Self-confidence
Verification	Evaluative ability	Affective pleasure in problem solving Cognitive integration of affect	Intrinsic motivation

FIG. 1.3.   Stages of the creative process and cognitive–affective processes.

affect-laden thoughts and openness to affect states would be important in the incubation stage and illumination stage; and affective pleasure in problem solving would be important in the illumination stage and verification stage. Cognitive integration of affect would also be dominant in the verification stage.

As divergent thinking has been identified as one of the central cognitive processes involved in creative thought, affective processes associated with divergent thinking are also central to creativity. This area is an appropriate place to begin our review of literature. One of the major literatures that theorizes about affect, divergent thinking, and creativity is the psychoanalytic literature. Specifically, the writing and research on primary process thinking and creativity offer numerous guidelines as to the role of affect in cognition. Chapter 2 reviews this work in detail.

2 Primary Process, Affect, and Creativity

The link between primary process thinking and creativity has been explored by numerous researchers and scholars over the years. The relationship between primary process and affect is a more recent question of great theoretical importance. It is important because if the link between primary process and affect can be articulated, then the primary process literature and the more recent empirical affect and cognition literature can be integrated. These two literatures fit together and can generate new ideas for future studies. Before looking at the relationships among primary process, affect, and creativity, we must first define primary process thinking.

This chapter reviews definitions of primary process thinking, the relationship between primary process and affect, the relationship between primary process and creativity, empirical findings with adults and children, and gives implications for the affect and creativity model discussed in chapter 1. In the model, primary process thinking is considered to be a subtype of affect-laden thoughts.

PRIMARY PROCESS THINKING

According to classical psychoanalytic theory, primary process thinking refers to drive-laden oral, aggressive and libidinal material and illogical thinking related to that material (Holt, 1977). Freud (1915/1958) first conceptualized primary process thought as an early, primitive system of thought that was drive-laden and not subject to rules of logic or oriented to reality. As Dudek (1980) stated, primary process is "the mechanism by which unconscious instinctual energy surfaces in the form of images or ideas" (p. 520). As the child develops, secondary process logical thinking becomes dominant and supplants primary process thinking. In normal child development, primary process thought becomes integrated into secondary process thought. Primary process content remains (aggressive, oral, sexual, anal) but in controlled, acceptable expressions. Another way of saying this is that a repressive barrier develops that controls the flow of this content into cognition.

As Holt (1977) defined it, primary process thought has content properties and formal properties. Primary process is expressed in primitive-aggressive and libidinal content, which reflects implied wishes. It also possesses formal characteristics such as illogical thinking, condensation (fusion of two ideas or images), and loose, associative links. Thus, we can refer to primary process content or to formal properties of loose associations and illogical thinking. Formal expressions and content expressions of primary process thinking may or may not go together.

Urist (1980) pointed out that the concept of primary process thinking has been an area of difficulty for those wishing to replace the energy model with other more contemporary approaches. Primary process has been a stumbling block because it is so based on the concept of instinctual energy. However it is an important construct that needs to be looked at in new ways and integrated into current theoretical approaches.

Recent conceptualizations of primary process have moved away from the energy model. Holt (1967), made a strong argument for using a structural model in the conceptualization of primary process thought. Holt proposed that primary process is a structure or group of structures, with its own course of development. Arieti (1976) and Suler (1980) proposed that primary process thinking may be a separate process that develops simultaneously with secondary process thought. Fischer and Pipp (1984) spoke of primary process as a separate process of thought that follows systematic developmental lines. Thus, primary process and secondary process thought would not be one continuum, but two separate dimensions. The concept of regression to an earlier mode of thought may not be necessary. The mechanism for access to primary process thinking may not be regression, but rather a different kind of process. Lazarus (1991) also spoke of primary process and secondary process thinking as parallel processes. Both operate in creative individuals in a well-integrated fashion.

PRIMARY PROCESS AND AFFECT

A very important theoretical question for the role of affect in the creative process is "what is the relationship between primary process thinking and affect?" The concepts of drive-laden and instinctual energy bring us into the realm of affect. In fact, Rapaport (1951) used the phrase *affect-charge* in discussing primary process thought. Primary process thoughts contain wishful content and/or instinctual passions. Even in Freud's (1895/1966) earliest writings in the Project in 1895, for example, primary process is discussed as a system of thought that is frequently accompanied by affect. Martindale (1981) said that primary process is a mechanism that is frequently used to deal with emotion-laden material. Zimiles (1981) discussed primary process as affect-laden cognition. Elkind (Alvin 1980) spoke of primary process as cognition guided by affect.

Russ (1987) proposed that primary process is a subtype of affective material in cognition. Primary process content is material around which the child had experienced early intense feeling states (oral, anal, aggressive). Current primary process content may reflect either current affect or a kind of "affective residue" in cognition left over from earlier developmental stages. This affective residue is associated with content around which the child at one time experienced early intense feeling states. This model is consistent with Rholes, Riskind, and Lane's (1987) discussion of mood-relevant cognition. Primary process content and memories were stored, or encoded, when emotion was present, sometimes intensely so. We come back to this point in chapter 7.

As mentioned earlier, primary process may also reflect a stylistic way of dealing with affective material—a kind of cognitive style. This is a concept that Pine and Holt put forth in 1960. These recent conceptualizations suggest that primary process is a cognitive-affective process that reflects a blending of cognitive and affective elements. Exactly how this translates into neurological processes remains to be determined. One possibility would be that affect and cognition are separate processes and that affect accompanies thoughts in primary process thinking. Zajonc (1980, 1990) would probably hold to this view. On the other hand, there may be more of a fusion of cognitive and affective elements in one process. This model is consistent with Bower's (1981) Associative Network Theory of Affect (see chapter 7 for a review of neurological theories). Whatever the mechanism, there is enough consensus in the literature to justify conceptualizing primary process thinking as a blend of affect and cognitive components. This point has not been emphasized very much in the literature. That is one of the reasons that the substantial literature on primary process thinking and creativity has been ignored by other branches of psychology, such as social psychology, in the affect and creativity area. The relationship between primary process and affect is not readily apparent, especially to researchers unfamiliar with psychodynamic theory. Once we see the connection between primary process and affect, then the theory and research become important and contribute to our understanding of the role of affect in the creative process. It is crucial that we begin to conceptualize primary process thought in terms of contemporary theories of affect and cognition. These new conceptualizations take the construct of primary process beyond the classic psychoanalytic instinctual drive model in a way that is theoretically useful and is consistent with the research that is investigating the relationship between cognition and affect.

REGRESSION IN THE SERVICE OF THE EGO AND CREATIVITY

Psychoanalytic theory has long postulated a relationship between access to primary process thinking in a controlled fashion and creativity. Kris' (1952) concept of "regression in the service of the ego" postulated that the creative individual can regress to this earlier mode of thinking. Following Kris' work, theorists (Arieti, 1976; Bush, 1969; Giovacchini, 1960; Suler, 1980) proposed that the concept of regression to an earlier mode of thought may not be necessary. The important concept is access to primary process content. Creative individuals may be more able to tap into the primary process and utilize the process in adaptive ways. Martindale (1989) put it well when he stated that "because primary process cognition is associative, it makes the discovery of new combinations of mental elements more likely" (p. 216). Because primary process is controlled, the individual can shift back and forth between this more primitive type of thinking and critical evaluative thinking. When one reads the psychoanalytic literature, one can see the similarities between primary process thinking and Guilford's cognitive processes involved in creativity. Guilford believed that the two processes most important to creativity were divergent thinking and flexibility of thought. Why would access to primary process facilitate divergent thinking or cognitive flexibility?

The psychoanalytic theory is based on Freud's (1926/1959) formulation that repression of "dangerous" drive-laden material leads to a more general intellectual restriction. Mobility and flexibility in the affective realm should generalize to more neutral thoughts and ideas. According to classical psychoanalytic theory, primary process thinking is characterized by "mobility of cathexis," that is, the energy behind ideas and images is easily displaced (Arlow & Brenner, 1964). There is a free flow of energy not bound by specific ideas or objects. In this mode of thinking, ideas are easily interchangeable and attention is widely and flexibly distributed. Thus, access to primary process material should increase the breadth of attention deployment and facilitate a fluidity of thought and flexibility of search among all ideas and associations. Thinking can then go off in different directions. It makes theoretical sense that primary process thinking relates to divergent thinking and to a flexible problem-solving approach. If recent conceptualizations that state that regression is not a necessary concept are accurate, then a more valid way of thinking about this issue is that access to primary process content and the ability to tap into the primary process itself facilitates divergent thinking and transformation abilities.

DESCRIPTIONS OF THE CREATIVE PROCESS

One of the ways to study the creative process is to listen to what creative people tell us. We said that access to primary process thought is hypothesized to be important in creativity. Specifically, psychoanalytic theory says that access to affect-laden primary process thinking should facilitate the kind of free association and broad scanning process important to divergent thinking, a major process in creativity. Divergent thinking is thinking that goes off in different directions and involves a free-ranging scanning of memories and associations. This scanning is necessary for disparate elements to be pulled together in new ways—resulting in a creative product. What does this free flow of associations look like?

One of the best examples to illustrate this kind of free flow of associations is a monologue by the comedian, Robin Williams. His improvisations illustrate this kind of free-associative flow of material. In commenting about the process, he said "And sometimes there are times when you're just on it—when you say the muse is with you and it's just flowing and that's when you know that the well is open again and you just put in the pipe and you stand back and say 'yes'. " He said " you're in control, but you're not— the characters are coming through you" (Culbane, 1988, pp. 5–14). This concept of being in control, but not in control, is common in the descriptions of the creative process by writers, artists, and so on. Williams also discussed his observations while observing his 4-year-old playing with rockets and using multiple voices. Williams said "that's it—that's the source" of one's creative process (Corliss, 1987, p. 75). If Williams was implying that early play involving primitive affect is an important determinant of creativity, then psychoanalytic theorists would agree with him. Psychoanalytic theorists hypothesize that it is access to primary process that is important to this free flow of ideas. If primary process is walled off, because it is dangerous, taboo-laden material, then it will interfere with the associative flow of material in general. An important theoretical question is whether or not all affective content functions in this way—or whether there is something unique about primary process content that is important to the creative process.

Other creative individuals also speak of the creative process in ways that implicate primary process thinking.

Poncaire (Ghiselin, 1952) in his 1913 essay on "Mathematical Creation" described the shifting images and ideas involved in the incubation stage of the creative process. He said that the picture is not thought out and determined beforehand. "Ideas rose in crowds. I felt them collide until pairs interlocked so to speak—making a stable combination" (p. 36). What Poncaire described here is the fluidity of thought that can occur in this free-ranging associative process. Also, the loosening of control is evident in this description. However, the importance of recognizing the solution through an evaluative process that recognizes the "stable combination" is also essential. Critical evaluation is necessary to recognize the solution when it occurs.

Jorge luis Borges, the Argentine writer, also described the feeling of not being in control. As Beard (1983) pointed out, Borges often used the passive tense in discussing his writing. Borges stated that:

> Suddenly I feel something is about to happen. Then I sit back and get passive, and something is given to me. I received a beginning and an end. When I have a subject, that subject tells me the style that he needs. When I write, I forget my own prejudices, my own opinions. The whole world comes to me. (pp. 7–8)

Yeats captured the dreamlike quality of this process by saying "when we are at the same time both asleep and awake, which is the one moment of creation" (Stallworthy, 1963).

In all of these descriptions, the similarity of the creative process to primary process thought is apparent. Primary process thought is dominant during sleep and is the process involved in dreaming. The illogical, loose associations that characterize primary process thought reflect the broad scanning and search process characteristic of divergent thinking. Often, primary process thought is equated with the unconscious. One thinks of creative individuals tapping into the unconscious. Vernon (1989) spoke of the role of unconscious processes. Creative thinking is differentiated from logical problem solving in that it involves "a greater degree of free-flowing imagination and recourse to subconscious activities such as incubation and inspiration" (p. 97). He concluded that these subconscious activities occur in both artistic and scientific work, although more frequently in artistic expression. Martindale (1989) made the point that primary process is not necessarily unconscious. Much of it is conscious thought. Individuals who can tap into this process in the waking state and who can also evaluate and synthesize when appropriate should have the advantage when it comes to generating a creative product. One is struck by the number of creative individuals who refer to the time between waking and sleeping, when one is drifting off in the hypnogogic state, as being a time when creative ideas come to them.

EMPIRICAL FINDINGS

Both theory and individual descriptions of the creative process suggest that primary process is important to creative thinking. What does the research literature suggest? In general, research findings support the theory that access to primary process thinking and creativity are related processes. Most of the research relies on Holt's Scoring System for Primary Process Responses on the Rorschach (Holt, 1977; Holt & Havel, 1960). Before discussing research findings, a brief review of Holt's scoring system is in order.

Holt (1977) believed that the Rorschach is uniquely suited to favor the emergence of primary process because (a) it calls for visual images, which is the preferred mode of operation for primary process thought, and (b) stimuli are ambiguous so there is more permission for any kind of content. Because there is much freedom in the task, one can assess the tendency of the individual to tap into primary process and to have access to affect-laden cognition. The Holt system scores the responses that contain primary process content (aggressive and libidinal that actually encompasses a broad range of affective content). The system measures the percent of primary process content in the Rorschach protocol and the effectiveness of the control of that content. A controlled response would express primary process content in a way that fits the form of the blot and is qualified in some appropriate way. For example, two talking bugs can be made into a more appropriate response by making them cartoon figures. It also measures formal characteristics of thought such as condensation and illogical associations. The scale was developed by Holt for use with adults. When used with children, the scale largely measures primary process content and adaptiveness of that content. Scorings of formal characteristics are a very small percentage in children's protocols (Dudek, 1975; Russ, 1982).

Holt's system yields four major scores. Intensity of primary process material is reflected in the Defense Demand score (DD). The DD Score is a 6-point rating scale for the intensity of the content. Cognitive integration and control of primary process material is reflected in the Defense Effectiveness score (DE). Form quality is a major determinant of DE, along with accompanying affect, control and defense scores, and overall clinical judgment of the response. Form quality tells us about the perceptual accuracy of the response. The DE score is rated on a 6-point scale from -3 to $+2$. For example, an adaptive, well-integrated response would be, on Card III, "two cooks stirring a pot of soup." In this response, oral content is permitted expression in a well-socialized response with good form quality. A poorly integrated response would be "the inside of the mouth with the voice box" to a vague area on Card VII. This time, oral content is expressed in a blatant fashion in an isolated body part of poor form quality.

The Adaptive Regression score (AR) indicates both the intensity of the primary process material and the effectiveness of the integration. The AR score best captures cognitive integration of affective material. "Two bears" on Card II, though well integrated, would have a relatively low AR score, whereas "two fighting, bloody bears" would have a higher AR score because of the intensity of the aggressive material. AR is determined by the formula $\Sigma(DD \times DE) / \#PPR$ where #PPR is the number of primary process responses in the total Rorschach protocol. The AR score has been the most frequently utilized score because it measures both the intensity of the content and the integration of the content. It is conceptualized as a measure of controlled access to primary process material. The term *Adaptive Regression* comes directly from Kris' (1952) concept of "regression in the service of the ego." There is an impressive body of validity studies for the AR score (Holt, 1977; Suler, 1980).

A fourth important score in Holt's system is the percentage of Primary Process material (%PP) in the Rorschach protocol. It is a measure of pure access to and expression of primary process material. Often overlooked, %PP has proven to be an especially important measure in research with children.

The Holt System measures both access to affect-laden material and the cognitive integration of that material. The four scores give information about different aspects of primary process thinking. Scores on Holt's system tell us whether an individual can allow drive-laden content to surface and then think about it. Can the individual tap into the primary process? Scores also tell us how well controlled and well integrated that content is in cognition.

There are numerous other scores in Holt's System. In fact, other theorists might argue that these other scores are major scores. However, most of the research studies with positive findings have utilized the four scores described earlier. Also, in terms of general reliability and robustness, these scores are the strongest, in my opinion. In my own research, I focus on %PP and AR as the major scores, which have been the most useful scores with child populations. Ultimately, researchers must use the scores that best reflect the constructs they are interested in measuring.

In adults, the AR score on the Rorschach has been significantly positively related to a number of measures of creativity (Cohen, 1961; Pine & Holt, 1960) and to problem-solving efficiency (Blatt, Allison, & Feirstein, 1969).

The AR score was related to divergent thinking in the Pine and Holt (1960) study and to the ability to make remote associations in a study by Murray and Russ (1981). Gamble and Kellner (1968) found that creative individuals had greater access to primary process. Dudek (1968) found more primitive primary process content (Level I in Holt's system) in artists than in nonartists and more primitive primary process in good artists then in poor artists. Dudek (1984) also found that top ranked creative architects produced more libidinal primary process content than lower ranked architects. See Holt (1977) and Suler (1980) for an extensive review of the adult literature.

RESEARCH WITH CHILDREN

In children, the same theoretical principles should apply. In the psychoanalytic literature, no distinction has been made between the role of primary process in creative thinking in adults and children. Children who can permit primary process material to surface in fantasy and play, in a controlled fashion, should be better divergent thinkers and more flexible problem solvers than children who have less access to primary process material. There is empirical support for this hypothesis. However, age, gender, and specific measures and scores utilized all emerge as important factors in the research studies.

As with adults, most of the studies in the child area used Holt's system for scoring primary process on the Rorschach. With children, the Holt system is scoring, for the most part, primary process content. Typical aggressive content in children's protocols would be fighting animals, monsters, exploding volcanoes, blood, and frightening insects. Typical oral content would be people eating, food, and mouths. In my research studies, the mean percentage of primary process content in the entire Rorschach protocol is about 50% in child populations.

Some of the first work that looked specifically at primary process (Holt's System) and creativity in children was that of Dudek (1975). She found no relationship between primary process thinking on the Rorschach and divergent thinking on the Torrance tests in fourth graders. She did find that primary process expression on a drawing task related to divergent thinking. Dudek concluded that the relationship between primary process and creativity is ambiguous in childhood, and that children have not yet learned to use primary process in adaptive ways. In a recent study by Dudek and Verreault (1989), creative children (fifth and sixth grade) gave significantly more total primary process ideation as measured by Holt's system as applied to the Torrance Tests of Creative Thinking. Also, more creative children demonstrated more effective use of regression in the service of the ego than noncreative children when popular responses were used to determine defense effectiveness.

Rogolsky (1968) found no relationship between the AR score and artistic creativity in third-grade children. However, a new adaptive regression score that combined amount of primary process with control measures for the entire Rorschach protocol (including populars) did significantly relate to artistic creativity for third-grade boys, but not for girls.

In Russ' research, in a series of studies (1980, 1981, 1982, 1988b) investigating primary process on the Rorschach and creativity in children, positive results were found. However, gender differences repeatedly occurred and different scores within Holt's system have been predictive of creativity in different studies. In the first study, Russ (1980) found a significant positive relationship between the AR score and reading achievement in second-grade children [$r(37) = .54$, $p < .001$]. This relationship remained significant ($r = .45$) after IQ was partialed out. The relationship also remained significant when productivity and general perceptual accuracy ($F + \%$) were partialed out. In a third-grade follow-up study with these children, the size of the relationship between third-grade AR scores and reading achievement remained consistent [$r(39) = .52$, $p < .001$] (Russ, 1981). Although reading achievement does not specifically speak to creativity, the underlying rationale for using this criterion was that children who had access to primary process thinking and integrated it well would be flexible problem solvers and open to ideas. Thus, they should be better learners than children with less access to primary process content. Several studies suggest the importance of flexible cognitive styles in the learning process. These studies on cognitive styles are important because if access to primary process facilitates cognitive flexibility, which in turn aids the learning process, then these better learners would have the advantage of accumulating a wide breadth of knowledge. A wide breadth of knowledge is important in creativity, as discussed in chapter 1. Ames and Walker (1964) found that indicators of cognitive flexibility on the Rorschach in kindergarten children were significant predictors of fifth-grade reading. They concluded that children with greater cognitive flexibility were open to information in the environment and could utilize cues better in learning situations. Smock and Holt (1962) found significant negative correlations between perceptual rigidity and school achievement, IQ, and curiosity. Heinicke (1969) found that children with reading problems significantly improved in their reading after psychotherapy. There were accompanying changes in what he called *ego flexibility* as measured by Rorschach determinants. His study suggested that, as the child develops more ego flexibility through psychotherapy, the learning process is effected. Ego flexibility included ratings of the child's capacity to express a variety of affects, to use a variety of defenses, and to use humor nondefensively. Of particular relevance to the primary process studies, children high in ego flexibility also showed a minimum repression of aggressive material.

Russ' next set of studies investigated the relationship between primary process thinking and the specific cognitive processes that Guilford hypothesized were important in the creative process — divergent thinking and transformation abilities (the ability to revise what one knows into new patterns and to think flexibly). Russ (1982) used two independent samples of third-grade children. Holt's scoring system for the Rorschach was the primary process measure. In order to have an adequate measure of flexibility of thinking for young children, Russ adapted the Luchins' Water-Jar Test (Luchins & Luchins, 1959). The Luchin's Water-Jar Test is an interesting task that taps a flexibility–rigidity dimension. The task requires the child to break out of an old set in solving a problem and to discover a new, more adaptive approach. The child must see new relationships in old patterns and be able to shift sets. There is some controversy in the literature (Guilford, 1967; Leavitt, 1956) as to whether this test actually taps a cognitive flexibility dimension. However, it does reflect the speed of cue utilization and the ability to give up an old approach for a new, more adaptive approach. The adapted version that I developed for this study is different from Luchins' standard version in that the problems are much simpler, instructions are given for the practice items and more direct cues are gradually built into the administration. Specifics of this task can be found in Russ (1982).

The results of this study found that for boys, the Adaptive Regression score was significantly related to flexibility of shifting sets in both samples of children. That is, the ability to express well-controlled primary process content on the Rorschach was related to the ability to shift problem-solving strategies. The fact that this result was replicated with a second sample of children is important. When samples were combined, the size of the correlation was $r(34) = .39, p < .01$. This relationship was independent of IQ. In addition, flexibility in shifting sets was significantly related to Iowa reading and composite achievement scores for boys (no relationship between the Luchins' and IQ). Adaptive Regression was also significantly related to achievement measures. This finding lends credence to the speculation that flexibility in problem solving is a factor in the learning process and in school achievement.

For girls, in both samples, AR was not related to the Luchins' task. In the second sample, the percentage of primary process was predictive of flexibility of shifting sets $[r(17) = .43, p < .05]$ for girls. The Luchins' Water-Jar Test proved to be reliable and valid in this study, and should be considered in future creativity research with children.

The relationship between divergent thinking and primary process was investigated in a fifth-grade follow-up study of 53 children who remained from the third-grade samples (Russ, 1988). Wallach and Kogan's (1965) adaptation of Guilford's Alternate Uses Test was the divergent thinking measure. A typical item is "how many different ways can you think of to use a newspaper." The score utilized in this study was the number of different categories of uses that were generated (spontaneous flexibility score). For example, to catch dripping paint, to wrap garbage in, and to make paper airplanes are all good and acceptable different categories of uses. The spontaneous flexibility score is a robust one that measures the ability to broadly scan associations and shift between different categories. As reviewed in chapter 3, this ability has been related to creative productions in children. The ability to scan associations should increase the probability of coming up with a new solution to a problem. The results in this study were significant for boys, but not for girls. Adaptive Regression and percentage of primary process were significantly related to the Alternate Uses Test for boys [$r(27) = .34, p < .05, r(27) = .33, p < .05$, respectively]. Primary process was not predictive of divergent thinking for girls.

In a recent study by Russ and Grossman-McKee (1990) with second-grade children, the same pattern of gender differences occurred. For boys, %PP on the Rorschach was predictive of divergent thinking on the Alternate Uses Test [$r(20) = .72, p < .001$]. This relationship was independent of intelligence. There was no significant relationship for girls. AR was not predictive of divergent thinking for either gender. It may be that in children this young, the frequency of primary process expression rather than the integration of primary process is the more important aspect of primary process in creativity. This is a point also made by Dudek and Verreault (1989).

The gender differences in the relationship between primary process thinking and cognitive processes thought to be important in creativity that occurred in the third-grade, fifth-grade follow-up, and second-grade studies are consistent with other studies in the adult and child literature. With children, Rogolsky's new adaptive regression score was predictive of artistic creativity for boys, not for girls. With adults, Holt (1977) stated that, in general, in studies that relate AR with creativity criteria, "negative findings from well-executed studies came entirely from samples of females" (p. 413). With adults, the relationship between AR and divergent thinking (Pine & Holt, 1960) and between AR and associational fluency (Murray & Russ, 1981) occurred for males, but not for females. Suler (1980), in a thorough review of the literature, also came to the conclusion that gender is an important moderator variable. When positive results do occur with female samples, the amount of primary process is the predictor. Pine and Holt (1960) concluded from their results with adult samples that the amount of primary process expressed was the better predictor of creativity in female subjects, whereas integration of primary process (AR) was the better predictor for males. In Russ' (1982) study with third-grade children, %PP did predict flexibility for shifting sets in the second sample of girls. On the other hand, %PP has also been a significant predictor of divergent thinking for second-and fifth-grade boys.

Other child studies have also found gender differences in the pattern of correlations between creativity tasks and predictor variables (Kogan, 1974, 1983). Kogan and Morgan (1969) and Wallach and Kogan (1965) found an inverse relationship between defensiveness and divergent thinking for boys, but not for girls. Boys who were more defensive did less well on the divergent thinking task. Kogan (1974) postulated an inhibition in scanning of internal memories and thoughts that effects both emotion-laden and nonemotion-laden material for boys.

A related finding is that in both samples in the Russ (1982) third-grade study, boys had a significantly greater percentage of primary process content than girls. This was specifically true for aggressive percepts. In the fifth-grade study, there was a trend ($p <$ .07) for boys to have a greater percentage of primary process responses. Kleinman and Russ (1988) also found that fourth-and fifth-grade boys expressed significantly more primary process content on the Rorschach than girls. These results are consistent with other studies in the child literature. Boys have consistently shown more aggression in their behavior and play (Maccoby & Jacklin, 1974). Girls recall fewer details of aggressive modeling (Bandura, 1965) and require longer tachistoscopic exposure time than do boys for the aggressive scenes (Kagan & Moss, 1962). Russ speculated that there may be more cultural taboos against expression of primary process material for girls than for boys (Russ, 1980). Even in these more feminist times, girls must continue to be "little ladies" in their expressions. Thus, girls may not learn to use these affective pathways in the development of other cognitive processes as effectively as boys. Because play is one of the major areas in which expression of affective material occurs, girls would be at a disadvantage. This point is discussed in more detail in later chapters.

It is important to point out that throughout the child creativity literature (Kogan, 1974), as well as in my own studies, there are few gender differences on any of the creativity tasks. The gender differences occur mainly in the pattern of correlations between predictors and creativity. However, in a recent study by Tegano and Moran (1989), third-grade boys had significantly more original responses on an ideational fluency test than girls. There were no gender differences in a preschool group. Tegano and Moran speculated that, by third grade, socialization may inhibit girls from taking risks and giving unusual responses

In reviewing the adult and child literature, one can conclude that controlled access to primary process thinking is an important dimension of creative thinking for males. For females, there are more negative results than positive, and those few positive results that exist occurred for the amount of primary process expressed. One possible explanation is that different aspects of primary process thinking are more important in creative thinking for girls than for boys. For girls, pure access to primary process content may be the important variable, whereas for boys, both access and integration are related to creativity.

Another possible explanation of negative results with female samples is that the Rorschach is not the best tool for assessing primary process thinking in girls. Girls offer fewer primary process responses. Inhibitions in the test-taking process may be a factor here for girls. Kogan (1974) speculated that differential effects of the testing situation may be partly responsible for the different correlates of divergent thinking for girls and boys. On the other hand, the AR score was predictive of school achievement in girls. Also, the amount of primary process expression on the Rorschach was predictive of affect and primary process in a play situation for both girls and boys (Russ & Grossman-McKee, 1990).

Because the Holt scoring system has been so heavily utilized in studies that have investigated primary process, a word about the merit of the test is in order based upon the previously reviewed studies. Russ (1987, pp. 147–148) outlined the advantages and disadvantages of the Holt system. With some alterations, they are listed here:

Advantages

1. It is a standardized measure of affective expression in fantasy. It is one of the few standardized instruments in the child fantasy and play area.

2. Children are comfortable responding to the Rorschach, especially when Exner's (1974) instructions are used.

3. Adequate inter-rater reliabilities have been reported in the literature for the major scores in the system. Holt (1977) reported coefficients of .56 to .94. Russ (1980) reported coefficients of .76 to .90.

4. There is a substantial body of validity studies in the literature. The AR score in particular relates to criteria that are consistent with theoretical predictions. The validity data exist mainly for male samples in both the child and adult literatures.

5. The Holt system is unique in tapping different aspects of primary process thought that are conceptually based. It is also possible to separate out cognitive from affective components.

Disadvantages

1. The Holt scoring system is cumbersome and difficult to learn and use. Much of the detailed information and a number of scores are not necessary for determining the major score in the system. For children, especially, the

system could be revised and simplified so as to be more feasible for use in large numbers of research studies.

2. Normative data for different age groups need to be obtained.

3. The system does not encompass all affective content categories, only those classified under primary process.

4. Test–retest and split-half reliabilities need to be established.

5. Holt's system needs to be related to other measures of affective expression of fantasy in children in order to build construct validity. The finding that primary process on the Rorschach does relate to affective expression and primary process expression in fantasy play is encouraging. (Russ & Grossman-McKee, 1990)

6. Questions remain as to the validity of the measure with female samples.

SUMMARY

In summary, there is a substantial body of research that suggests that access to affect-laden primary process thinking is related to cognitive processes important to creativity for males. Specifically, referring back to the model of affect and creativity in chapter 1, primary process thinking relates to divergent thinking and to transformation abilities in males. The results are consistent with different samples and researchers. For females, the results are mixed. There are a few studies that find that access to primary process is related to creativity. One possible explanation of the gender differences may be that females do not have as much access to primary process thinking as males do, and that this restriction somehow effects the development of the relationship between primary process and creativity in girls. Another possibility is that the major measure of primary process thinking used in the literature, Holt's system for the Rorschach, may not be a valid and appropriate measure for females.

A crucial theoretical question is whether the role of primary process in the creative process is similar for males and females. The primary process literature suggests that there may be differences. We need to look at other literatures and other measures for a clearer picture. Chapters 3 and 4 look at affect, primary process, and creativity in the children's play literature.

3 Children's Fantasy, Play, Affective Expression, and Creativity

Another major literature that speaks to affect and creativity is the children's fantasy and play literature. Kogan (1983) stated that "the research directed toward the issue of the play–creativity linkage may well represent the most promising set of findings in the children's creativity literature over the past decade" (p. 642). Although the theoretical link between play and creativity has existed for quite a while, the empirical evidence has been building only since 1970. The creativity, fantasy, and play areas are especially important because of the cognitive-affective links that can be investigated. Affective and cognitive processes both contribute to creativity and fantasy responses and to play behavior.

Children's play is important because play is the arena in which children express two of the affective processes thought to be important in creativity—affect-laden thoughts and affect states. Practice in expressing a variety of affect-laden fantasies and affect states should enhance the development of creative cognitive processes and of these affective processes themselves. In this chapter, there is a review of the literature on play and cognitive processes; methodological issues in play and creativity research; play and affective processes; and types of affective expression in play and creativity.

PLAY AND COGNITIVE PROCESSES

There is a substantial body of research in the area of children's use of fantasy, play, and cognitive functioning (Dansky, 1980; Fein, 1981; Singer,

1973). Sherrod and Singer (1979) identified a cluster of processes involved in fantasy and pretend play activities: the ability to form images; skill in storing and retrieving formed images; possessing a store of images; skill in recombining and integrating these images as a source of internal stimulation and divorcing them from reality; and reinforcement for skillful recombining of images. They state that it is the last two processes that are unique to fantasy and play activity. These last two processes involve transformation abilities and, probably, divergent thinking abilities.

Klinger (1971) concluded that there is agreement in the literature that play and fantasy have a common origin. There are similar processes involved in both functions. Piaget (1945/1967) wrote of fantasy as "interiorized play." On the other hand, Singer (1981) conceptualized play as the externalization of fantasy. Play, then, is an expression of internal fantasy. Vygotsky (1930/1967) believed that creative imagination originated in children's play (Smolucha, 1992).

Singer and Singer (1990) suggested areas of cognitive development that are facilitated by pretend play activities. Play helps the child to (a) expand vocabulary and link objects with actions, (b) develop object constancy, (c) form event schemas and scripts, (d) learn strategies for problem solving, (e) develop divergent thinking ability, and (f) develop a flexibility in shifting between different types of thought (narrative and logical).

The relationships among fantasy, play, and creative problem solving have been important areas for empirical investigation. It is here that we are beginning to learn about the specific processes involved in fantasy that relate to other cognitive processes. Saltz, Dixon, and Johnson (1977) found that fantasy play facilitated cognitive functioning on a variety of measures. They speculated that fantasy play is related to cognitive development because of the involvement of representational skills and concept formation. Sherrod and Singer (1979) stressed the importance of viewing fantasy play and cognition as a transactional system—each facilitating the other. Singer and Singer (1976), in a review of the literature, concluded that the capacity for imaginative play is positively related to divergent thinking, verbal fluency, and cognitive functioning in general.

Wallach (1970) stressed the importance of the relationship between divergent thinking and fantasy. Divergent thinking, as discussed in chapter 2, is thinking that goes off in different directions and is thought to be an important component of the creative process (Guilford, 1959). Subjects who scored well on divergent thinking tasks produced novel stories on the TAT (Maddi, 1965) and engaged in daydreaming activity (Singer, 1973). Wallach (1970) posited that breadth-of-attention deployment is the underlying variable involved in divergent thinking tasks, such as in Guilford's Alternate Uses Test ("how many uses for a brick?"). As Kogan (1983) pointed out, breadth-of-attention deployment refers to a scanning of the environment and memory in an associational manner. It is this variable, breadth-of-attention deployment, that both divergent thinking and fantasy activity may share. This variable would account for the play–creativity link, from a cognitive perspective.

Play has been found to facilitate divergent thinking in preschool children. Dansky and Silverman (1973) found that children who had opportunities to play with objects gave significantly more uses for those objects than did control subjects. Play opportunities increased divergent thinking productions. In a later study, Dansky (1980) found that make-believe play was the mediator of the relationship between play and divergent thinking. Free play enhanced associative fluency, but only for children who engaged in make-believe play. Also in the second study, the objects in the play period were different from those in the test period. Thus, the play had a generalized effect.

Dansky's theoretical assumption for the hypothesis that make-believe would facilitate associative fluency was that the process of free combination and mutual assimilation of objects and ideas involved in play is similar to the elements involved in creative thinking. Dansky (1980) speculated that the free symbolic transformations inherent in make-believe play helped create a temporary cognitive set toward the loosening of old associations. This is consistent with the work of Sutton-Smith (1966). Sutton-Smith stressed the role of play in the development of flexibility in problem solving. Play provides the opportunity to explore new combinations of ideas and to develop new associations for old objects. The object transformations that occur in play help to develop the capacity to see old objects in new ways. Kogan (1983) also suggested that children's play behavior involves a search for alternate modes of relating to the object, a process similar to searching for alternate uses for objects in divergent thinking tasks.

If new configurations, new solutions, and new ideas can occur during a temporary loosening of old associations in children, then similar events should occur for adults. If we can find adult equivalents of children's play, such as day-dreaming, fantasizing, and other forms of symbolic play, then new configurations could occur for adults.

METHODOLOGICAL ISSUES IN PLAY AND CREATIVITY RESEARCH

A number of methodological issues arise in the play and creativity research. Smith and Whitney (1987), in a carefully executed study, failed to confirm the hypothesis that play would enhance divergent thinking in preschool children. Smith and Whitney took careful precautions against experimenter bias. One of their conclusions was that previous positive results that linked play experiences to divergent thinking were due to experimenter effects. In previous studies that used an experimental approach, the same examiners administered the play experience and the associative fluency task. Smith and Whitney proposed that "unconscious experimenter bias during testing was possible in each study" (p. 50).

Although the results of the Smith and Whitney study raise an important issue and suggest that previous studies should be interpreted with greater caution, it is too soon to totally dismiss the results of those studies. There are several important methodological issues that need to be addressed.

First, it is difficult to introduce a new examiner into the experiment for the divergent thinking task, as Smith and Whitney did, without interfering with the experimental set one is trying to induce. One of the major theoretical rationales for hypothesizing that play would facilitate associative fluency is that play, especially make-believe play, results in a temporary cognitive set that loosens old associations (Dansky, 1980). Imaginative play should increase breadth-of-attention deployment, which increases the range of internal scanning of ideas and associations. For this loosened set to occur, young children, especially, must feel relaxed and comfortable with the examiner. The procedure of having one examiner create the permissive play set and a new examiner administer the creativity task could easily interfere with the effect of the play condition. In the Smith and Whitney (1987) study, in addition to a new examiner, the children were taken to a different room for the divergent thinking task. The physical movement, ensuing conversation, and time delay all could have disrupted the loosened cognitive set.

This methodological issue presents a dilemma for future researchers. In order to precisely control for examiner effects, the phenomena under investigation could be seriously interfered with. There are two possible solutions that come to mind. One is to continue using the same examiner for both tasks but to be extremely careful about standardized administration of the divergent thinking task. It is easy to administer divergent thinking tasks in a standardized manner and control for verbal cues. Indeed, one would assume that at least some of the previous experimental studies utilized a careful, standardized approach to task administration. It is more difficult to control for nonverbal cues, but side-by- side seating might be one way to eliminate facial cues. A second possible solution would be to use different examiners for the two tasks, but to use a procedure that protects against breaking the experimentally induced play cognitive set. The new examiner could trade places with the first examiner so that there would be no room change or time lapse (N. Kogan, personal communication, April 3, 1987). Also, time to become familiar with both examiners, which Smith and Whitney did build into their study, is crucial. In addition, examiners who carry out these studies should be individuals with whom children feel comfortable.

A second methodological issue is how the variable of make-believe is assessed and/or manipulated. Dansky's (1980) study is the major study with which Smith and Whitney compare their results. However, a major difference between the Dansky study and the Smith and Whitney (1987) study is their treatment of the variable of make-believe play. Dansky had hypothesized that the free-play condition would facilitate divergent thinking for make-believe players but not for non-make-believe players, when compared with imitation and problem-solving groups. This hypothesis was confirmed. Make-believe was treated as a moderator variable. On the basis of pre-experimental observations and ratings made in natural free-play situations, children were designated as players (high make-believe percentage) or nonplayers (low make- believe percentage). The natural individual differences on the dimension of make-believe were focused on. As Dansky stated "situational variables interact with specifiable individual differences among children (player/nonplayer) to yield a particular mode of activity (make-believe), which then has implications for the level of associative fluency displayed" (p. 578). In the Smith and Whitney study, make-believe was treated differently. It was manipulated during a separate make-believe condition which consisted of a 2- minute period of encouraged pretend play, followed by the instructions "Let's pretend that these things can become anything that you want them to." Six children each in the make-believe and free-play conditions were monitored and it was determined that significantly more make-believe did occur in the make-believe condition. Smith and Whitney (1987) found no significant differences in associative fluency among make-believe, free-play, or imitation groups. The differences in the results of the Dansky study and the Smith and Whitney study could as easily be explained by the lack of comparability in the treatment of the make-believe variable as by the experimenter bias issue. Artificial manipulation of make-believe may not result in the same kind of construct as is reflected in the child's natural tendency toward engaging in make-believe play. It is also possible that the make-believe play condition enhanced make-believe play and/or divergent thinking only for the children who were good make-believe players to begin with. Make-believe may have functioned as an unexplored moderator variable in the Smith and Whitney study as it had in the Dansky study.

There are a significant number of correlational studies in the literature that report a relationship between play and divergent thinking. Singer (1973), Kogan (1983), and Singer and Singer (1990), provided reviews of this important literature. A number of these studies did control for experimenter effects in that play observations and divergent thinking task administration were carried out by different examiners. Using this approach, Singer and Rummo (1973) and Lieberman (1977) found relationships between dimensions of play and divergent thinking in kindergarten children. Also Russ and Grossman-McKee (1990) and Russ and Peterson (1990) found significant relationships between play and divergent thinking in first- and second-grade children (reviewed in chapter 4).

Another major methodological issue in the play and creativity literature is that of the adequacy of the divergent thinking test measures. Kogan (1983) and Runco (1991) have excellent reviews of this literature. Both concluded that the commonly used measures of divergent thinking, such as the Wallach and Kogan version of the Alternate Uses Test, are respectable and valid measures. Runco (1991) discussed scoring issues and different subscores of divergent thinking tests. Milgram (1990) also concluded that measures of divergent thinking are valid and that divergent thinking is an important component of talent. However, she supported the trend in creativity research to focus more on real-world products. This is a growing trend and is discussed in chapter 9.

The two major theoretical variables proposed as mediating variables between play and creative problem solving have been the capacity to form new combinations of ideas and breadth-of-attention deployment. These are mainly cognitive variables. There has been little attention given to possible affective variables that may account for the relationships among play, fantasy, and problem solving. Affect as a variable has not been explored much in the experimental play and creativity literature. It is possible that various dimensions of affect function as moderator variables in the relationship between play and divergent thinking. The different ways in which affect interacts with make-believe could differentially effect divergent thinking. This factor might partially account for the mixed results in the play literature.

The results of the Smith and Whitney study do raise an important note of caution about the play–creativity experimental paradigms. However, the relationship between play and divergent thinking is a complicated one that involves a number of different cognitive and affective dimensions that cannot be addressed definitively by one or two studies. Rather, there needs to be a series of studies, both correlational (concurrent and longitudinal) and experimental, that build converging evidence about the nature of the relationship between play and creativity.

AFFECTIVE PROCESSES IN PLAY AND CREATIVE PROBLEM SOLVING

In general, there has been little empirical investigation of affective processes in children. As Masters, Felleman, and Barden (1981) pointed out, the empirical study of affective expression in children is a young area. Most of what we know about affective expression has been learned through two sources, observations of children's play and measures of children's fantasy. The development of reliable, standardized, and valid measures has been difficult. The lack of adequate measures has been one of the reasons that cognitive processes, not affective processes, have been the focus of play research. Rubin, Fein, and Vandenberg (1983) described this phenomenon as the "cognification" of play.

Singer and Singer (1990) discussed imaginative play within a cognitive-affective framework and proposed it as a "central conception from which we can explore the nature of imaginative play and its role in childhood" (p.29). They reviewed Tomkin's (1962, 1963) model of affect and proposed that play is reinforcing when it permits expression of positive affect and the appropriate control of negative affect.

One of the problems in the play literature is that there are no commonly used, standardized measures of affective expression in children's play. Most researchers developed their own play observation measures (Howe & Silvern, 1981; Lieberman, 1977; Singer, 1973). Singer's (1973; Singer & Singer, 1981) research is one of the major bodies of work in the area of make-believe play and its correlates. In his studies of children's play, he emphasized systematic measurement of play samples. Singer (1973) pointed out the necessity to focus on specific variables with a rather narrow focus on play. Once the investigator decides which dimensions are important, he stresses the need to identify specific behavior samples, to stay with observable behaviors, and to train raters carefully. Singer himself has specifically focused on the variable of imagination in play. He also developed 5-point rating scales for measuring positive affective expression, concentration, and mood. Singer and Singer (1981) also included dynamic themes in play such as danger and power, which were rated as present or absent. Instructions for the rating of these variables can be found in Singer (1973) and Singer and Singer (1981). Milos and Reiss (1982) devised a rating scale that measured separation themes in play and desire to master the problem. Howe and Silvern (1981) developed a Play Therapy Observation Instrument, which is a broad-based instrument that rates a number of different dimensions in children's play. There is a fantasy play dimension, although affect in fantasy does not appear to be rated. Most measures have not specifically focused on affective content themes in fantasy play. A standardized measure of affective expression in play would be useful in creativity research. The need for this kind of scale was one of the reasons we developed the Affect in Play Scale described in chapter 4.

Types of Affective Expression in Play and Creativity

Affective expression in fantasy play is an important dimension of cognitive-affective functioning. Before a standardized measure could be developed, a classification system for type of affect in fantasy was necessary to provide conceptual guidelines for the instrument. In play, feeling states are expressed in fantasy in a variety of ways. Although no formal classification system had been developed, three dimensions of affective expression in fantasy emerged in the play and psychotherapy literature: (a) actual affective experiencing and expression of feeling states and emotions (affect states); (b) affective content themes in fantasy productions such as aggression, fear, and pleasure (affect-laden fantasy); and (c) cognitive integration and modulation of affective material. Thus, affective expression in play can be classified as emotional expression and expression of feeling states, affective content in fantasy (emotional and primary process themes), and cognitive integration of affective material. The classification scheme presented here is one attempt to identify different types of cognitive affective processes reflected in fantasy. The conceptual basis of the Affect in Play Scale is discussed in chapter 4. The first two categories, affect states and affect-laden thoughts are the major two affective processes related to creativity presented in the Affect and Creativity Model in chapter 1. Cognitive integration of affective material is another major category in the model.

Affect States.   The first type of affective expression is actual expression of the feeling state itself in fantasy play. The psychotherapy literature refers to this as catharsis—the release of emotions and expression of feelings. Catharsis has long been thought to be therapeutic (Axline, 1947; A. Freud, 1965). Moustakas (1953) pointed out that expression of negative emotions is especially beneficial. Permission to express unacceptable feelings during play therapy has been viewed as a major mechanism of change in the psychotherapy process (Freedheim & Russ, 1983, 1992).

In terms of how actual emotional expression and experiencing might affect cognitive functioning, most research has investigated the effect of cognition on affect, not affect on cognition (Masters et al., 1981). For example, Schachter and Singer's (1962) classic work illustrated that cognition influences feeling states. Masters et al. (1981) discussed one experimental paradigm for investigating the effect of affect on cognition—the affect-induction procedure. As developed by Mischel, Ebbesen, and Zeiss (1972), children are asked to think affectively valanced thoughts, that is, "think about something that's fun." Children recall and think about an experience that is associated with a particular emotion. Facial expressive behavior and self-report measures offer validation for the assumption that induced affective states produce natural affective states (Masters, Barden, & Ford, 1979). Using the affect-induction procedure, induced positive affective states influenced problem solving and learning (Masters et. al., 1979). They found that induced positive affective states significantly enhanced speed and accuracy on a discrimination task in preschool children. Negative affective states significantly retarded learning. They pointed out that although actual mood states in children may be transient, moods may influence cognitive functioning.

Alice Isen's findings with adults are consistent with these results and have implications for the child area. Isen et al. (1987) found that inducing positive affect states facilitated creative problem solving. They concluded that positive affect states increase the tendency to combine material in new ways and to see the relatedness between divergent stimuli. Isen's work is discussed in detail in chapter 6. The research paradigm that she uses is an appropriate one for child research.

Play may be one real-life example of self-induced affective states. Children conjure up feeling states and play out a variety of themes and affects. If so, and if affective states in play can be validated as being similar to natural affective states, then play would be an ideal situation in which to investigate the effect of affective expression on creative functioning. The fact that Masters et al. (1979) found that negative affective states retarded learning seems inconsistent with the psychotherapy literature, which thinks of emotional expression as beneficial. Perhaps short-term effects of affect on cognition differ from long-term effects.

Lieberman's (1977) work pertains to affective expression in play and cognitive functioning. She focused on the variable of "playfulness," which included affective components of spontaneity and joy. She found that playful kindergarten children did better on divergent thinking tasks than nonplayful children. Singer and Rummo (1973) found a relationship between playfulness and creativity in kindergarten boys. There was no relationship for girls. Lieberman postulated that playfulness is a linking variable between play and creativity. The playfulness in play is a forerunner of the recombining of ideas involved in the creative process. The positive affect involved in playfulness may be an important variable here. Singer & Singer (1990) reported that positive affect was related to imaginative play.

Affect-Laden Thoughts. A second type of affective expression in fantasy play is the expression of affective content. Themes of affective content or primary process material are expressed in play. Emotion may or may not accompany the content. In this category, both affective and cognitive elements are involved. Play is a major vehicle for forbidden affective content to be thought about. Primary process material can also be expressed and integrated. As Waelder (1933) said, play is a leave of absence from reality. It is a time to let go and allow primary process thinking to occur.

We can think of play as a kind of practice with the free association process. It is a mix of divergent thinking and affect. Winnecott's work is important in understanding the role of play in creativity. As Winnecott (1971) pointed out, play is a deeply pleasurable process that involves instinctual material. He stated that in play "the child puts out a sample of dream potential" (p. 51).

A major goal of many forms of therapy with children is to free-up their thinking about affective material—to make dangerous thoughts not so dangerous, so that cognitive functioning in general is not so constricted. One of the basic tenets of psychodynamic psychotherapy is that constriction in the affective fantasy sphere will constrict cognitive functioning in other spheres. This was the theoretical foundation for my work, reviewed in chapter 2, which found that children who had greater access to primary process material and could integrate it well were better school achievers and more creative thinkers. Singer and Singer (1981) found that preschoolers rated as high imagination players showed significantly more themes of danger and power than children with low imagination. These themes would be rated as primary process themes by Holt's system of categorization. They suggested that play may serve as a medium for "reenacting" conflicts and concerns for highly imaginative children.

Saltz et al. (1977) found that preschoolers who engaged in fantasy play over a period of time showed better cognitive development than children who did not engage in play. The most effective play condition was the thematic-fantasy play condition that involved the most imaginative play. Traditional fairy tales were acted out in this condition. Saltz et al. speculated that one reason for the effectiveness of this condition was the importance of acting out the conflictful themes of the fairy tales. Affective involvement may have been an important variable in facilitating cognitive functioning.

Cognitive Integration of Affective Material. A third type of cognitive-affective variable is cognitive integration and modulation of affective material. This is a broad global category that refers to how the child cognitively deals with affect and conflictual material. This category is mainly a cognitive one, which probably includes a number of cognitive processes. For example, how well is the affective material integrated into fantasy play? This type of cognitive integration would be similar to Holt's DE score for primary process on the Rorschach. Sarnoff (1976) stated that the effective use of fantasy reflects a cross-situational, cognitively based structure that results in the ability to modulate the expression and experience of otherwise disruptive emotions. The Adaptive Regression score in Holt's system might reflect this more general ability to deal with conflict-laden affective material. Sarnoff's conceptualization is consistent with Erikson's (1963) concept of mastery in play. Children use play to gain mastery over traumatic events and everyday conflicts. Play is a major form of conflict resolution. Waelder (1933) described the child as repeating the unpleasant experience over and over, until the child gains mastery over the experience. Play is a "method of constantly working over, and, as it were, assimilating piecemeal an experience which was too large to be assimilated instantly at one swoop" (p. 218). The unpleasant affect associated with the event is no longer unmanageable. The child has turned passive into active and mastered the event. The child has "digested" the event, to use Waelder's analogy. Play is an assimilative process. Waelder has described here the "working through" process, which is a major mechanism of change in psychotherapy (Freedheim & Russ, 1983, 1992). The child slowly gains access to conflict-laden material and plays it out until the conflict has been resolved.

It is probable that the working through process helps develop cognitive structure that further aids the child in assimilating future stressful events. In this way, how children handle affect partially determines cognitive structure and, therefore, functioning in a variety of areas. The ability to use play and integrate affect should increase the ability to cope with stressful situations and to utilize "regression in the service of the ego," which is so important in creativity.

The three aspects of affect in fantasy described here serve as a conceptual base for a play observation instrument — The Affect in Play Scale (Russ, 1987; Russ & Grossman-McKee, 1990). The development of this scale and its relationship to creativity is reviewed in the next chapter. One of the major uses of the scale could be to explore the role of play, and of affect in play, in the development of creative thinking abilities.

4 The Affect in Play Scale

The need for a reliable and valid scale that measures affective expression in children's fantasy play has been widely documented (Howe & Silvern, 1981; Rubin et al., 1983). Partly to meet that need and partly to develop an instrument that could serve as an alternative for children to Holt's Scoring System for Primary Process on the Rorschach, the Affect in Play Scale was developed. A standardized measure of affect in play is useful in creativity research. It enables us to investigate the relationships among affective processes in play and creativity as well as the effect of interventions with affect-laden thoughts and affect states on creativity. A measure of affective expression in play taps a wider range of affective content than the Holt Scoring System for Primary Process on the Rorschach and may prove to be a more valid measure for girls.

This chapter reviews the Affect in Play Scale. It discusses the standardized play task, the scoring system, reliability of the scale, validity studies in the creativity area, validity studies in the adjustment area, and future research directions. The scale consists of a play task and criteria for a rating scale. The conceptual basis for the scale is discussed in chapter 3. (This subject was also examined by Russ in 1987.)

THE PLAY TASK

It is important that the play objects and task to be observed be unstructured enough so that individual differences in fantasy play can emerge. The play task utilizes two neutral looking puppets, one boy and one girl, and three small blocks that are laid out on a table. It is administered individually to the child. The play task is appropriate for children from 5 to 10 years of age. The instructions for the task for the free-play period are:

> I'm here to learn about how children play. I have here two puppets and would like you to play with them any way you like for five minutes. For example, you can have the puppets do something together. I also have some blocks that you can use. Be sure to have the puppets talk out loud. The video camera will be on so that I can remember what you say and do. I'll tell you when to stop.

The child is informed when there is 1 minute left. If the child stops playing during the 5-minute period, the prompt, "You still have time left, keep going" is given. The task is discontinued if the child can not play after a 2-minute period.

These instructions are free-play instructions that leave much room for the child to structure the play and present themes and affects that are habitual to him or her. Although the instruction "For example, you could have the puppets do something together" provides structure, we found that some structure was necessary for many children to be able to carry out the task. These instructions can be altered to elicit different types of affect. For example, to pull for aggression, the instructions would be "Play with them and have the puppets disagree about something," rather than "Play with them anyway you like." The play task described here is appropriate for grades 1–3. In our experience, many kindergarten children have difficulty with the puppet task. However, the rating criteria could be used in a natural play observation situation for very young children.

For older children, although the scale has not been used with these groups, we expect that the children would feel self-conscious in engaging in puppet play more suitable for younger children. However, if asked to put on a "puppet show" or a play, then the task may be appropriate for grades 4–6 as well. In a pilot study, fifth-grade children were comfortable with the "put on a play with the puppets" instructions.

THE RATING SCALE

The Affect in Play Scale measures the amount and types of affective expression in children's fantasy play. It also measures cognitive dimensions of the play, such as quality of fantasy and imagination. Affective expression consists of the occurrence of affective content themes and actual emotional expression. Conceptually, the Affect in Play Scale taps three dimensions of affect in fantasy:

1. Actual affective experiencing through expression of feeling states (affect states).
2. Affective content themes, including primary process themes (affect-laden fantasy).
3. Cognitive integration of affect. This dimension is reflected in the combination of quality of fantasy scores and affect scores.

All three categories of affect are included in the affect and creativity model in chapter 1.

Both Holt's Scoring System for Primary Process on the Rorschach (1977) and Singer's (1973) play scales were used as models for the development of the Affect in Play Scale. In addition, the work of Izard (1977) and Tomkins (1962, 1963) was consulted to ensure that the affect categories were comprehensive and covered all major types of emotion expressed by children in the 4–9 age group. There are eight major scores for the Affect in Play Scale.

1. Total frequency of units of affective expression. A unit is defined as one scorable expression by an individual puppet. In a two puppet dialogue, expressions of each puppet are scored separately. A unit can be the expression of an affect state, an affect theme, or a combination of the two.

2. Variety of affect categories. There are 11 possible affective categories, the last 6 of which are primary process categories. The categories are: Happiness/Pleasure; Anxiety/Fear; Sadness/Hurt; Frustration/Displeasure; Nurturance/Affection; Aggression; Oral; Oral Aggression; Anal; Sexual; Competition.

3. Mean intensity of affective expression (1–5 rating). This rating measures the intensity of the feeling state or content theme.

4. Mean intensity × frequency score.

5. Comfort in play score (1–5 global rating).

6. Global quality of fantasy (1–5 rating).

7. Mean quality of fantasy, based on subscores of organization, elaboration, imagination, and repetition.

8. Affective integration scores:
   a. Mean quality & mean intensity;
   b. Mean quality x frequency;
   c. Mean quality & mean intensity × frequency.

The scale manual and the criteria for the intensity of affect ratings, comfort, and quality ratings are presented in Appendix A.

The Affect in Play Scale measures the occurrence of eleven affective content categories. The last six categories, aggression, oral, oral aggression, anal, sexual, and competition are primary process categories. Any verbal or physical expression that reflects a content category is scored as one affective unit. The total frequency of affect score is the total number of affective expressions during the session. Intensity of affective expression for each unit is rated on a 5-point Likert-type scale. For example, one puppet telling the other puppet "I don't like you" receives an aggressive content score and an intensity score of 3. If the statement were accompanied by a punch, it would receive an intensity score of 4. Another dimension scored is variety of affective content, which is the total number of categories of affect expressed. Children's general comfort in play, as indicated by enjoyment and involvement, is rated on a 5-point scale by the examiner. To assess the quality of the fantasy productions themselves, ratings on a 5-point scale are obtained for organization, elaboration of plot, redundancy, and imagination. The imagination score measures the novelty of the fantasy expression, the use of pretend play, and removal from daily experience of the activities. The mean of these four cognitive dimensions is the mean quality of fantasy score. A global rating of quality of fantasy is also obtained. This global rating was included to provide a check on the mean fantasy score. These two scores are very highly correlated. In the development of the scale, there was an attempt to separate the affective dimensions from the more cognitive quality of the fantasy. Theoretically, there should be at least two separate dimensions, one cognitive and one affective, in children's fantasy play. A combined score, the integration of affect score, is the sum of the total mean quality and mean intensity multiplied by frequency of affect score. This score was thought to reflect both affective expression and quality of fantasy, and to be comparable to the Adaptive Regression score on the Rorschach. Several different score combinations are utilized in capturing integration of affect.

To summarize, the major scores on the Affect in Play Scale are total frequency of affect, variety of affect categories, mean intensity of affect, intensity × frequency score, comfort in play, global quality of fantasy, mean quality of fantasy, and integration of affect (quality + intensity × frequency).

The primary process categories can be rated or not, depending on the theoretical bent of the investigator. Also, a positive affect score and negative affect score can be obtained.

VALIDITY STUDIES

Once the Affect in Play Scale was constructed, pilot studies were carried out to ensure that the task was appropriate for young children and would result in adequate individual differences among normal school populations (Russ, Grossman-McKee, & Rutkin, 1984). By 1984, the basics of the task and scoring system were in place. Recent studies have resulted in refinement of the scoring criteria and a shortening of the play period (from 10 minutes to 5 minutes). The next step was to build construct validity for the scale through a series of validity studies. Four major validity studies have been carried out with the Affect in Play Scale, which are reviewed later. These studies investigate the relationships among affect in play and creativity, measures of adjustment and self-esteem, and the factor analytic properties of the scale.

Affect in Play Scale, Primary Process on the Rorschach, and Divergent Thinking

The first study by Russ and Grossman-McKee (1990) investigated the relationships among the Affect in Play Scale, primary process thinking on the Rorschach, and divergent thinking in first- and second-grade children. Sixty children individually received the Rorschach, Affect in Play Scale, and Alternate Uses Test. Holt's Scoring System was the measure for the Rorschach.

Interrater reliabilities for the play scores were good. Based on 15 randomly chosen subjects, Pearson -r correlation coefficients were as follows: total frequency of affect, $r = .90$; variety of categories, $r = .82$; intensity of affect, $r = .53$; mean quality of fantasy, $r = .88$; imagination, $r = .74$; and comfort, $r = .89$. With the exception of intensity of affect, which was therefore not included in the analysis, all of the interrater reliabilities were judged to be adequate.

As predicted, amount of primary process thinking on the Rorschach was significantly positively related to the amount of affect in play (see Table 4.1). Total frequency of primary process on the Rorschach was significantly positively related to the following play measures: frequency of affect [$r(44) = .34, p < .01$]; variety of affective categories [$r(44) = .44, p < .001$]; frequency of primary process affect [$r(44) = .30, p < .05$]; frequency of non- primary process affect [$r(44) = .26, p < .05$]; comfort [$r(44) = .45, p < .001$]; quality of fantasy [$r(44) = .48, p < .001$]; imagination [$r(44) = .47, p < .001$]; and the composite integration of affect score [$r(44) = .37, p < .01$]. Percentage of primary process, which controls for general productivity, was also significantly related to most of the play variables, although the correlations were lower than those with total frequency. Percentage of Primary Process was significantly related to frequency of affect [$r(44) = .32, p < .05$]; variety of affective categories [$r(44) = .28, p < .05$]; frequency of primary process [$r(44) = .28, p < .05$]; frequency of nonprimary process [$r(44) = .25, p < .05$]; quality of fantasy [$r(44) = .27, p < .05$]; imagination [$r(44) = .30, p < .05$] , and integration of affect [$r(44) = .32, p < .05$].

TABLE 4.1
Pearson Product-Moment Correlations Among Rorschach and Affect in Play
Measures for Total Sample

Rorschach	Affect in Play Scale							
	Freq. of Affect	# Categ. of Affect	Com- fort	Freq. of Primary Process Affect	Freq. of Non- primary Process Affect	Quality of Fantasy	Imagin- ation	Integra- tion of Affect
Freq. of primary process	.34**	.44***	.45***	.30*	.26*	.48***	.47***	.37**
% primary process	.32*	.28*	.23	.28*	.25*	.27*	.30*	.32*
Adaptive regression	.11	.14	.005	−.009	.26*	.02	.07	.06
Adaptive regression × # primary process responses	.25*	.41**	.31*	.16	.28*	.21	.23	.22

$n = 46$.
*$p < .05$. **$p < .01$. ***$p < .001$.

Primary process thinking on the Rorschach was equally predictive for girls and for boys in the play situation. The relationships between the variables were not affected when intelligence was controlled for. Contrary to prediction, the Adaptive Regression (AR) score on the Rorschach, which taps the combined intensity and integration of primary process material, was not predictive of play behavior. One possible explanation is that the construct of integration of primary process as reflected in perceptual accuracy on the Rorschach is different from what is reflected in the quality of fantasy in play. However, when frequency of primary process responses was not controlled for in the AR score, this new composite score ($AR \times f$) related to some of the play categories, such as comfort.

The major finding in this study, that primary process expression on the Rorschach is significantly related to affective expression in children's play, is important because it shows that there is some consistency in the construct of affective expression across two different types of situations.

A second major finding of this study was that affective expression in play was predictive of divergent thinking (see Table 4.2). The predicted relationships between the play scores and the Alternate Uses test were all significant for the total sample, except for that between frequency of nonprimary process affect and divergent thinking. Divergent thinking was significantly related to frequency of affect [$r(58) = .42$, $p < .001$], variety of affect

TABLE 4.2
Pearson Product-Moment Correlations Among Primary Process and Affect
Measures and Alternate Uses Test

| | Alternate Uses – # Categories Score | | |
	Total Sample	Boys	Girls
Rorschach[a]			
% primary process	.50***	.72***	.27
AR	−.17	−.09	−.27
Ar × # primary process responses	.10	.34	−.21
Affect in play scale[b]			
Frequency of affect	.42***	.40*	.44**
# Categories of affect	.38**	.56**	.29
Comfort in play	.23*	.36*	.22
Frequency of primary process affect	.41***	.38*	.48**
Frequency of non-primary process affect	.20	.20	.22
Quality of fantasy	.30**	.48**	.32*
Imagination	.35**	.40*	.44**
Integration of affect	.42***	.45**	.38*

[a]$n = 46$ for total, $n = 22$ for boys, $n = 24$ for girls.
[b]$n = 60$ for total, $n = 30$ for boys, $n = 30$ for girls.
*$p < .05$. **$p < .01$. ***$p < .001$.

categories [$r(58) = .38, p < .01$], comfort [$r(58) = .23, p < .05$], frequency of primary process affect [$r(58) = .41, p < .001$], quality of fantasy [$r(58) = .30, p < .01$], imagination [$r(58) = .35, p < .01$], and integration of affect [$r(58) = .42, p < .001$]. All correlations remained significant when IQ was partialed out, due to the fact that IQ had such low relationships with the play scores (e.g., $r = .09$ with frequency of affect, $r = -.01$ with comfort, $r = .08$ with quality, and $r = .12$ with imagination). The fact that intelligence did not relate to any of the play measures is theoretically consistent with the theoretical model for the development of the scale and is similar to the results of Singer (1973).

There were no gender differences in the correlations between the Affect in Play Scale and the Alternate Uses test. Again, in this study, there were gender differences in the correlations between the Rorschach and divergent thinking. As in previous Rorschach studies, reviewed in chapter 2, primary process expression on the Rorschach was predictive of divergent thinking for boys, but not for girls. Gender differences have also occurred in the play and creativity literature (Lieberman, 1977; Singer & Rummo, 1973). Positive relationships between play and creativity measures have occurred more frequently for boys than for girls.

One explanation for the lack of gender differences in the relationship between play and creativity could be that the medium of puppet play is a more natural form of expression for girls than other forms of play or test situations. Another possible explanation is that a wider range of affect categories and forms of expression are expressed in play than on the Rorschach. Thus, the play scores may reflect the girls' true ability for access to and expression of affective material and primary process material. These results suggest that the Affect in Play Scale has the potential to be an equally valid measure for boys and girls.

An interesting finding in this study was that primary process affect was significantly related to divergent thinking, whereas nonprimary process affect was not. The difference in the size of the correlations was significant. This finding was not specifically predicted, but is consistent with psychoanalytic theory that focuses on the importance of primary process thought in the creative process. Theoretically, it is access to dangerous, taboo-laden primary process material, around which the individual has experienced conflict, that is facilitative of divergent thinking. Repression of this uncomfortable content inhibits the creative process. Although the present study says nothing about facilitation of divergent thinking, the fact that only primary process relates to divergent thinking, for both boys and girls, is noteworthy and suggests some future research directions.

Affect in Play Scale, Divergent Thinking, and Coping

A study by Russ and Peterson (1990) investigated the relationships among the Affect in Play Scale, divergent thinking, and coping in school in first- and second-grade children. The main purpose of this study was to obtain a large enough sample size (121 children) so that a sound factor analysis of the play scale could be carried out for the total sample and separately for boys and girls. A second purpose was to replicate the result of the Russ and Grossman-McKee study that found a positive relationship between affective expression in play and divergent thinking. In addition, the relationship between play and coping was explored.

One hundred twenty-one children (64 boys and 57 girls) were individually administered the Affect in Play Scale and a Coping in School scale. In a separate testing session, with a different examiner, they were administered the Alternate Uses test. The Affect in Play Scale used in this study and subsequent studies was slightly different than the earlier version used in the Russ and Grossman-McKee study. The play period was 5 minutes instead of 10 minutes. A video camera was used rather than a tape recorder. Also, some of the affect categories were condensed, because of infrequent occurrence. Displeasure and frustration became one category and sadness and hurt became another category. A new category, competition, was added because of its prevalence in children's play and because it is considered to be a derivative of aggressive content in Holt's system. Finally, there were some minor adjustments in the intensity rating criteria.

An important theoretical question is whether or not affect in fantasy and the cognitive components in fantasy are separate processes or one process. The theoretical assumption underlying the play scale was that at least two separate processes are involved—one cognitive and one affective. In the development of the scale, care was taken to make the scoring criteria of the affect scores separate from the cognitive dimensions. For example, the intensity rating of an aggressive expression should not be influenced by the amount of imagination in the play; the scoring of affective expressions themselves should be independent of the quality of the fantasy. Also, the scoring of imagination should not be influenced by the amount of affect in the response. Thus, if only one underlying dimension were identified in a factor analysis, it would probably not be due to an artifact of the scoring system.

A factor analysis of the total sample was carried out using the principal component analysis with oblique rotation. Seven major scores for the Affect in Play Scale were included in the factor analysis. (Scores that involved statistical combinations of scores were not included in this particular factor analysis.) An oblique solution, using the method default (Cattell & Jaspers, 1967) yielded two separate factors as the best solution (see Table 4.3). The first and dominant factor appears to be a cognitive factor. Imagination, organization, quality of fantasy, and comfort in play significantly loaded on this first factor. The second factor appears to be an affective factor. Frequency of affective expression, variety of affect categories, and intensity of affect loaded on this second factor. Although separate factors, there is a significant amount of shared variance ($r = .76$), suggesting that the factors also overlap.

TABLE 4.3.
Oblique Factor Structure of the Affect in Play Scale for Total Sample

Play Scores	Cognitive	Affective
Frequency of affect	− .27	.79
Variety of affect	.00	.60
Mean intensity	.12	.40
Comfort	.55	.06
Quality of fantasy	.62	.04
Organization	.69	− .09
Imagination	.65	− .08

Note. $N = 121$.

When factor analyses were carried out separately for girls and boys, similar factor structures emerged. For boys, the factor structure replicated that of the total sample. For girls, the only difference from the total sample was that intensity of affect loaded on the cognitive factor.

The important finding here is that affective expression and cognitive expression in fantasy play, though related, also have significant amounts of unique variance, which suggests that there are separate processes involved.

Another important finding in this study was that the Affect in Play Scale was significantly positively related to divergent thinking. These results replicated the findings of the Russ and Grossman-McKee (1990) study with children of the same age. As in the previous study, there were no gender differences in the pattern of correlations. For the total sample, divergent thinking was significantly related to frequency of total affect [$r(115) = .26$, $p < .01$]; variety of affect [$r(115) = .25$, $p < .01$]; comfort [$r(115) = .37$, $p < .001$]; quality of fantasy, [$r(115) = .43$, $p < .001$]; imagination [$r(115) = .42$, $p < .001$]; primary process [$r(115) = .17$, $p < .05$]; non-primary process [$r(115) = .24$, $p < .01$]; and integration of affect [$r(115) = .30$, $p < .001$]. These relationships remained significant when IQ was partialed out.

Based on this study, we can say with more confidence that affective expression in fantasy relates to divergent thinking, independent of the cognitive processes measured by intelligence tests. Also, the affective measures on the play scale form a separate factor from the cognitive elements of fantasy play. We are beginning to distil the affective elements from the cognitive elements, a necessary step for future research. One of the next major research questions is whether we can demonstrate that experimental manipulation of affective processes will effect creative thinking.

It is important to note that in both the Russ and Grossman-McKee (1990) study and the Russ and Peterson (1990) study, the significant relationship between play and divergent thinking occurred in studies where the administration of the play task was carried out by a different examiner than for the divergent thinking task. Given Smith and Whitney's (1987) criticism that previous positive results that linked play and associative fluency were due to experimenter effects (see chapter 3), these are important findings. Nothing can be said yet about causation, but the Affect in Play Scale provides a tool for investigation in studies that look at the effect of different affective conditions on divergent thinking.

In this study, we also looked at the internal consistency of the play scale. Split-half reliability for frequency of affective expression, comparing the 2nd and 4th minutes with the 3rd and 5th minutes of the play period, was $r = .85$ using a Pearson product- moment correlation coefficient. This reliability coefficient is very adequate.

PLAY AND COPING

Although not the focus of this book, the relationship between play and coping and adjustment is briefly reviewed. The link between creativity and adjustment is further discussed in chapter 5. Children who utilize play well should be better adjusted and be better problem solvers than children who are not expressive in play. The Affect in Play Scale provides a tool for measuring different processes in play and should be predictive of criteria that make sense theoretically, such as coping and adjustment. For the Russ and Peterson (1990) study, we included two measurers of coping. One was the frequently used Zeitlin Coping Inventory (1980), which is a teacher's rating scale. The other was a 12-item self-report measure that we developed for this study. The scale measured how children would deal with typical problems that arise in the school situation. We rated the number of acceptable solutions to a problem and quality of the response on a 1-3 scale. For example, one item was "what would you do if you forgot your lunch?" We hypothesized that good players would be good copers. The ability to use play well, work through problems, and integrate affect should increase coping ability.

The results for the total sample showed significant positive correlations of low magnitude between the cognitive scores on the play scale and coping ability. The affective scores did not relate to coping ability. For example, quality of fantasy play was significantly related to the number of good coping responses on the Coping in School scale [$r(119) = .30, p < .001$] and to the Zeitlin scale [$r(119) = .20, p < .05$]. Imagination was significantly related to the Coping in School scale [$r(119) = .35, p < .001$] and to the Zeitlin scale [$r(119) = .25, p < .01$].

An interesting finding was that divergent thinking ability was related to coping in school [$r(115 = .21, p < .01$] and to the Zeitlin [$r(115) = .32, p < .001$]. This finding is consistent with that of Russ (1988b) with a fifth-grade sample in which divergent thinking was significantly related to the Zeitlin [$r(27) = .58, p < .01$]. These findings suggest that divergent thinking ability, so important in creative thinking, may also be a component in coping and problem solving in everyday living.

A one-year follow-up on a subsample of 50 of the original 121 children was carried out by Peterson (1989). We focused specifically on the ability of the Affect in Play Scale to predict self-esteem, over a one-year period. Major scores on the play scale were predicative of self-esteem on the Self-Perception Profile for Children (Harter, 1985). The social acceptance, physical appearance, and global self-worth subscales of the Self-Perception Profile for Children were most consistently related to play. In addition, self-esteem was positively related to the amount of positive affect in play and negatively related to negative affect in play.

Affect in Play Scale and Pain Complaints

Grossman-McKee (1989) investigated the relationship between Affect in Play and pain complaints in 89 first- and second-grade boys. Her major hypothesis was that there would be a significant negative relationship between amount of affect expressed in play and the number of pain complaints in children. She based this hypothesis on the psychodynamic conceptualization that children who are unable to deal with negative emotions through fantasy are more likely to internalize these emotions and develop somatic symptoms.

Grossman-McKee found, as predicted, a significant negative relationship between amount of affect expressed and the number of pain complaints reported by the boys [$r(89) = -.33, p < .01$] and by their parents [$r(81) = -.25, p < .05$]. She concluded that children who complained more frequently of headaches, stomach aches, limb pain, or chest pain were less able to express affect in play and were less able to cognitively integrate the affect into play.

In addition, a number of the play scale scores were significantly negatively related to state anxiety as measured by the State–Trait Anxiety Inventory for Children (STAIC) (Spielberger, 1973). That is, children who were better players showed less state anxiety on the STAIC.

Another interrater reliability check was carried out in this study. For 16 subjects, the correlations were very good. For frequency of affect, $r = .96$, quality, $r = .90$, organization, $r = .73$, imagination, $r = .91$, and comfort, $r = .94$. The only reliability deemed to be inadequate was for mean intensity, $r = .24$.

STABILITY OF AFFECT IN PLAY SCALE SCORES

The means of some of the major scores of the Affect in Play Scale for the three major studies just reviewed are comparable (see Table 4.4) Note that in Study 1, the length of the play session is twice as long as in Studies 2 and 3. One half of the total frequency of affect units expressed would be 12.3 units, which is comparable to the two 5-minute-period studies. This indicates that the stability of the scores is good when different populations of first- and second-grade children are used. The average first and second grader expresses 11 to 13 separate affective expressions in puppet play during a 5-minute period. An average of three to four different categories of affect are expressed.

TABLE 4.4
Means and Standard Deviations for the Affect in Play Scale Across Studies

	Study 1[a] (Russ & Grossman-McKee, 1990)		Study 2[b] (Grossman-McKee, 1989)		Study 3[c] (Russ & Peterson, 1990)	
	M.	*S.D.*	*M.*	*S.D.*	*M.*	*S.D.*
Frequency of affect	24.7	23.61	13.01	21.40	10.99	10.33
# Categ. of affect	4.8	3.07			2.97	2.02
Comfort	2.4	1.6	2.33	1.50	2.96	1.3
Quality of fantasy	2	1.3	2.27	.93	2.7	1.29
Imagination	2.03	1.3	1.90	1.1	2.58	1.3

[a]10 minute play period.
[b]5 minute play period: boys only.
[c]5 minute play period.

EXAMPLES OF AFFECT IN PLAY SCALE DIALOGUE

Excerpts from the first 90 seconds (approximately) of play dialogue for four children are presented here. All of these children are girls in the first or second grade. All express some affect in their play, but there are major differences in the amount of affect expressed. The dialogue is always between the puppets. On the video tapes, we can code the nonverbal expressions and affect tone of the verbal expression. The verbal transcripts presented here can not adequately reflect the affect dimensions but do give a sense of how these children differ in affective expression.

PLAY TRANSCRIPTS — PUPPET DIALOGUE

Child #1: High Affect/High Quality of Fantasy

— Let's build a tall building. I'll put this top on (build with blocks).
— No, I want to.
— No, I am.
— Hey, I said I was — give me those (tussle).
— I want to.
— No, I do. (knock it down)
— Oh no — we'll have to start all over thanks to you.
— it wasn't my fault, it was your fault.
    (a block fell)

- Oh—I better go get that block—it fell down the stairs.
- Now you have me put that on top or I'll tell mom.
- Ah—what did I do?
- Be my sister.
- OK—but we will both build a building - I put 2 on and you put on 1 since you get to put on the top.
- Fair enough.
- Uh oh. (blocks fell)
- I'll straighten this out.
- We built a tall building. (with glee)
- What should we do now?
- I don't know.
- Let's build a playground.
- The playground is boring. (with feeling)
- no—it isn't there are lots of fun things to do there.
- I always hit my hand and get scratches and scrapes.
- Well maybe if you were more careful, that wouldn't happen.

Child #2: Moderate Affect/High Quality Fantasy

- Oh Boo Hoo Boo Hoo. I don't have anyone to play with. Boo Hoo. I'll just play with my blocks and maybe that will make me feel better. (Building)
  I'll stack this there and this here and stack this there—that's about as tall as me.
  Um—that makes me feel better—I'm happy—ha ha ha.
  Maybe I'll go to my friend Sally's house.
  (knock)
- Who is it?
- It's Rebecca, remember, your friend.
- Hi Rebecca, come in.
- HI Sally.
  I wanted to know if I can play with you.
- Ok—you can play with me—anytime you want, if I'm home. (laugh) do you want to go to the playground?
- Oh sure Sally but I don't know how to get there.
- Oh Rebecca (with feeling) I do—you can just follow me. We'll play and jump rope ok?
- ok Sally.
- Here is the playground—I think or this might be a school.
- Oh what—what day is it—it's Saturday, so we don't have school— Here's the playground.

— Oh remember, we were going to play Miss Lucy.
— yes — ready. (play and sing)

Child #3: Lower Affect/Lower Quality of Fantasy

— Hello little girls — want to play with these blocks?
— Ok — let's build something.
— Ok.
  (Build)
— Uh oh. (blocks fell over)
— We'll build it again.
  (build)
— There.
— Let's make a picnic table.
— There.
— Now let's play — let's build a tunnel.
— ok.
— let's go under the tunnel.
— let's build some monkey bars.
— let's play house — I'll be the mother.
  (Much of the time was spent building — no verbalization.)

Child #4: Lower Affect/Lower Quality of Fantasy

— Hi Sara — How are you doing?
— Fine.
— Can I come over to your house?
— yes you can.
— Well — one day I'll come over to your house and play with you too.
— For now let's play with the blocks.
  (build)
— That's good Sara.
— Can you make something else?
— yes I can.
— thank you.
  (build)
— That's good.
— Well I can make something different.
  (build)
— That's good too — but I can make something very different.
  (build)
— That's good too — but that isn't so good — watch this.

— That's good too — it's very hard — so you did a hard one.
— yes, I did.

FUTURE RESEARCH DIRECTIONS WITH THE AFFECT IN PLAY SCALE

The Affect in Play Scale is proving to be a reliable and valid measure of fantasy and affect in children's play. The results of the validity studies are encouraging. The scale is a comprehensive measure of children's affect and fantasy. It appears to be valid for both girls and boys. In two studies, affect in play has been related to a divergent thinking measure. The next research steps will be to investigate the relationship between affect in play and other creativity criteria. Amabile (1990a) stressed the importance of utilizing actual products as criteria of creativity. Ratings by experts of children's drawings or stories could be used as a measure of creativity in addition to creativity tests. Milgram (1990) found children's use of leisure time to be predictive of creative performance. Longitudinal data is also important to obtain. Is affective expression in children's play predictive of creativity over time?

Researchers need to continue investigating the robustness of the individual scores of the scale. In the actual coding of the scale, the 1–5 intensity rating is the most time consuming dimension to score. It is difficult to achieve adequate interrater reliability for this score, although we did so in the Russ and Peterson (1990) study. For many research questions, the intensity score could be eliminated from the coding. All of the other scores, including the occurrence of an affective unit and coding for affect category, are relatively easy to score.

Another line of research in the creativity area is to use the scale to investigate the affect of altering affective states and affective content themes on cognitive processes important to creativity. By varying the instructions for the play task, one can use the Affect in Play Scale to assess the effectiveness of the instruction in altering affect. The dependent variables would be divergent thinking or transformation ability. In a Master's Thesis by Grossman-McKee (1985), different instructions did result in increased aggressive content and increased happiness content. So there is evidence that altering instructions alters types of affect expressed in the play.

Studies need to investigate whether divergent thinking and transformation ability can be altered by altering the affective expression in play. This play instruction research paradigm is an alternative to the mood-induction paradigm (Isen et al., 1987) discussed in chapter 6.

The mood-induction paradigm may be more appropriate for investigating affect states and the play-instruction paradigm more appropriate for investigating affect-laden content. Both paradigms should be used to investigate the differential effects of positive and negative affect on creativity. The different effects of positive and negative affect on creativity is one of the current important theoretical questions in the field. Different research paradigms and different measurement tools are necessary to study it.

The Affect in Play Scale provides a way of assessing affect in play and, hopefully, will prove to be beneficial to the fields of creativity research and of psychotherapy research.

CONCLUSIONS – PLAY, AFFECT, AND CREATIVITY

What are our conclusions about how the affective processes in play aid in developing creative thinking?

We can conclude from the research and clinical literature that play helps the child deal with affect in a variety of ways. Play helps the child:

1. Express affect and develop the ability to experience and express emotions as they arise.

2. Express and think about affect themes. Affect content and primary process content is permitted to surface and be expressed through play. Over time, the child develops access to a variety of memories, associations, and affective and nonaffective cognition. This broad repertoire of associations helps in creative problem solving.

3. Resolve conflicts and master the many traumas of daily life. Affective material is explored in depth. Again, the child is freer to have access to a variety of affect states. Affective content does not get repressed and become unavailable.

4. Develop cognitive structure that enables the child to contain and modulate affect. Future conflicts and stressors can then be more easily handled. This cognitive structure should also help the child to "regress in the service of the ego" and use primary process adaptively.

5. Experience positive affect which is part of the play experience. Positive affect has been found to be important in creativity.

6. Practice with the free flow of associations that is part of divergent thinking.

We can speculate that, over time, the child who uses play well develops the habit of being open to affect and emotions and of actively working on problems. We need to empirically demonstrate that openness to affect states and affect themes facilitates divergent thinking and flexible problem solving. The specifics of the mechanisms need to be worked out and other dimensions identified. The Affect in Play Scale is one tool for accomplishing these goals.

5 Personality Trait Approach to Creativity

Much of the research in psychology in the creativity area has focused on the relationship between personality traits and creativity. The studies have usually been of two types. The first type looks at personality characteristics of creative individuals. The second approach investigates relationships between measures of specific personality traits and measures of creativity.

This chapter reviews the main personality characteristics found to be impoitant in creativity; links between these personality traits and affective processes; creativity and adjustment; artistic and scientific creativity; and the role of passion in creativity.

The most comprehensive review of the personality trait research, with a specific focus on traits of creative individuals, is that of Barron and Harrington (1981). They concluded that the research of the previous 15 years is consistent with earlier findings in the field in the research programs of Barron (1969), MacKinnon (1965), Roe (1953), and Cattell and Butcher (1968). Barron and Harrington (1981) listed a set of core characteristics of creative individuals that emerge in different domains. The core characteristics are: high valuation of aesthetic qualities in experience, broad interests, attraction to complexity, high energy, independence of judgement, autonomy, intuition, self-confidence, ability to resolve antinomies or to accommodate apparently opposite or conflicting traits in one's self-concept, and a firm sense of self as "creative" (p. 453).

Martindale (1989) integrated the issues involved in the personality and creativity research well when he stated that "creative cognition occurs only within a certain configuration of personality traits" (p. 213). I would add that this configuration increases the probability that certain affective processes will occur that then effect creative cognitive processes. The possession of specific personality traits sets the stage for specific affective processes to occur. In turn, specific affective processes are reflected in some personality traits. Comfort with affect states and affective fantasy should increase the probability that certain personality traits would develop.

In choosing the list of personality traits for the affect and creativity model (Fig. 1.2), I chose those traits that emerged from major research programs, that were found in several research studies, that were consistent with Barron and Harrington's list, and that theoretically could have some link with affective processes. I also avoided redundancy where possible. For example, broad interests in the Barron and Harrington list is really subsumed by wide breadth of knowledge, a generally recognized cognitive variable. Also, autonomy and independence of judgement are similar characteristics.

The following list of personality traits are those I included in the model as being most important and linked to affective process. Two characteristics listed under the personality trait section in the model, curiosity and intrinsic motivation, might be better conceptualized as motivational systems. These characteristics are discussed in chapter 6.

PERSONALITY TRAITS, AFFECT, AND CREATIVITY

At this time, we can only speculate about which personality traits might relate to which affective processes or might be partial reflections of those processes. It is probable that only a small portion of the variance in these rather global personality traits is accounted for by affective components.

Openness to Experience

McCrae and Costa (1987) evolved a 5-factor model of personality. The one factor in their 5-factor model that relates to creativity is openness to experience. They found that interest in a variety of experiences for their own sake, in a variety of domains such as fantasy, aesthetics, feelings, actions and values was related to divergent thinking and other creativity measures. They conceptualize openness to experience as a mode of processing experience (McCrae & Costa, in press). Openness to experience is a basic dimension of personality and can be conceptualized in structural and motivational terms. McCrae and Costa (in press) stated that "artists can be considered prime examples of individuals high in openness to experience." Artists demonstrate many of the characteristics that have been found to correlate with the openness to experience dimension. McCrae and Costa have a full review of the literature and list the following personality characteristics as correlates of the openness to experience factor: unconventional, perceptive, empathic, flexible, high need for change, variability in mood, wide range of interests, variety of mood states, tolerance of ambiguity, preference for complexity, and sensation seeking. The openness to experience factor relates to divergent thinking (McCrae, 1987) with correlations around .40.

In regard to affect, McCrae and Costa concluded that open individuals have more access to thoughts, feelings, and impulses than non-open individuals. They discussed tolerance of ambiguity as being an important characteristic, enabling a variety of thoughts and feelings to be experienced simultaneously. They also discussed the importance of access to primary process in facilitating openness to experience.

Tolerance of Ambiguity

Tolerance of ambiguity and the ability to simultaneously consider opposing views, even about the self, is a frequently cited characteristic of creative individuals (McCrae & Costa, in press; Vernon, 1970). The ability to tolerate ambiguity and to avoid premature closure keeps the search process and the attempt to resolve the problem open. More alternative solutions can be tried. Sternberg (1988) described the successive approximation process of scientific problem solving. One needs to hold the problem open and avoid coming to a solution too early. Also, being able to tolerate ambiguity would enable the individual to see a problem and identify problems. And, as McCrae and Costa (in press) pointed out, tolerance of ambiguity permits different types of affect to be experienced simultaneously.

Independence of Judgement and Unconventional Values

Independence of judgement and unconventional values are common characteristics of the creative individual. Csikszentmihalyi and Getzels (1973) found that artists were uninterested in social norms and social acceptance. Creative individuals can go their own way and not be so influenced by societal norms. This quality would be important in determining sensitivity to problems and in having the courage of one's convictions to pursue a course of action or project.

Preference for Challenge and Complexity

Barron's (1969) early work demonstrated a preference for complexity in both artists and scientists. Voss and Means (1989) discussed the role of affect in the preference for challenge. They stressed the negative affect involved in seeing the problem and implied that the anticipation of the positive affect involved in solving the problem is the motivating force. However, the negative may not be so negative. The tension involved in seeing the challenge may have exciting, positive aspects.

Heinzen (1989) found that moderate challenge in a job-hunting task facilitated creative ideation in college students. Runco (in press) proposed that some kind of tension must precede intrinsic motivation and the creative act. Tension can evolve from a number of sources, either intrapersonal or interpersonal. One kind of tension is explained by Festinger's (1962) cognitive dissonance theory in which an individual is motivated when there is a tension between different sources of information. As Runco conceptualized it, the affective tension that is stirred when a gap exists in a problem or situation is highly motivating. The affect would also serve as a cue for problem identification.

Self-Confidence

Self-confidence has been found to be associated with creativity in a number of studies. Gough (1979) found that it was a commonly chosen adjective among creative individuals when describing themselves.

Self-confidence is important in helping the individual to persist in a task and to tolerate criticism and repeated failure before a creative solution occurred. Sternberg (1988) pointed out the number of false starts that are involved in creative problem solving. Creative individuals often had to tolerate criticism and much worse and to persist in their work in spite of this. As Martindale (1989) pointed out, high levels of self-confidence are important during this process. Shaw (1989, in press) also described the need for creative scientists and engineers to tolerate rejection, criticism, and intense negative affect.

Risk Taking

The tendency to take risks increases the likelihood that one would engage in behaviors and have experiences that would broaden the individual's knowledge base. Barron (1988) stressed the importance of risk taking in creativity. Sternberg (1988) emphasized the importance of good judgement in determining the acceptable level of the risk taken.

Gender Differences

Some gender differences emerged in the personality literature. Helson (1990) did important work on creative women at Mills College. She found that creative college women had been selected as special by their families

(1968). In a follow-up study, those women who succeeded did not have brothers (1985). This finding occurred again in a study of creative women mathematicians (1971). This is an important finding in light of Albert's (1980) conclusion that the importance of being the first born or only son in achieving eminence has been repeatedly demonstrated. Thus, in Helson's work, it was only when boys were absent that the girl could be invested in in such a way that she could develop the personality resources necessary to achieve success.

Helson also found that creative women did not inhibit negative affect. This is an important finding in light of the mood-induction and primary process research.

Gough (1988), in using his Adjective Check List for ratings by observers, found that creative women were rated as being different from creative men. Some items formed a cluster only for men and fit the typical cluster of creative adjectives (adventurous, ingenuous, artistic, versatile, original). For women, a different cluster emerged (thoughtful, playful, reliable, persevering, responsible, fair-minded, and logical). This is not the typical description of the creative person. Much of the personality research has been done with male samples. The creative women in Gough's study look more conventional on the surface. One might speculate as to what this means. Perhaps creative women learn to stifle their more innovative, unconventional personality qualities in social situations. Or perhaps unconventional personality qualities are simply not good predictors of creativity in women.

CREATIVITY AND ADJUSTMENT

If we conceptualize creativity as evolving from a configuration of personality and affective processes that set the stage for creative acts to occur, then the propensity for adjustment could go either way, depending on the mix of processes. If creative individuals are good divergent thinkers, have diverse associations, have access to primary process in a controlled fashion, are open to affect states, and are good critical thinkers, then one would expect them to be sensitive but relatively stable individuals, perhaps with periods of emotional instability. The Woody Allen figure of his early movies comes to mind—highly sensitive, open, anxious, and "neurotic," but basically well-functioning, stable, and creative.

The research evidence continues to grow in the area of adjustment and creativity. Some studies are supportive of the hypothesis that creative individuals are adaptive and well-adjusted. Cropley (1990) pointed out that many of the psychological traits that relate to creativity are also indicators of positive mental health. Other studies point to a relationship between creativity and psychopathology. Prentky (1989) has an excellent overview and discussion of creativity and psychopathology. Prentky stated that "a genetic predisposition to certain forms of mental illness may be associated with a cognitive style similar to that which promotes creativity" (p. 244). He conceptualized in an information processing model. There is a similarity between mentally ill individuals and creative individuals in how information is processed. Studying cognitive processes of the mentally ill can help with understanding creative processes.

Prentky (1989) reviewed a number of studies that look at the question of creativity and adjustment. He quoted Lange-Eichbaum (1932) who found that many artists became psychotic after their major work was completed. Prentky reviewed clinical and biographical data on a number of creative individuals and concluded that affective disturbances tend to predominate, especially for artists (writers, composers). He also concluded that if writers are disturbed, the disturbance is likely to be affective (Andreasen & Canter 1974; Jamison 1988). Jamison (1989), in a convincing study of British artists and writers, found that 28% of the sample sought treatment for mood disorders. This finding is consistent with Mitchell's (1972) conclusion that writers respond to experience with greater sensitivity than the average person, and therefore, suffer more. Drevdahl and Cattell (1958) found that creative artists were stable, but emotionally sensitive and living under strain. Research with scientists paints a different picture. Roe's (1951, 1952) scientists were independent and self-sufficient. MacKinnon's (1965) architects were a well-adjusted group, adaptive and open-minded. Stein (1971) found that scientists gave evidence of emotional well being. Cattell (1966) concluded that creative scientists may be a more emotionally stable group than creative artists.

Richards (1990) and Richards and Kinney (1990) reviewed the creativity and health area. Richards (1990) offered three major conclusions:

1. Mild psychopathology may contribute to creativity. For example, one finds elevated creative accomplishment in individuals with mild mood swings. She concluded that mild mood elevations may carry advantages for creativity.

2. Intermediate levels of variables may be most optimal for creativity (moderate anxiety or challenge).

3. Affect is important in creativity. Richards stressed the positive affect involved in creative accomplishment. Consistent with this conclusion is Schulberg's (1990) finding that deficits in experiencing pleasure are negatively correlated with creativity.

Much has also been written about schizophrenia and creativity. McNeil (1971) found that relatives of schizophrenics had a higher degree of creativity. There was an association between divergent thinking ability and psychoticism (Claridge, Canter, & Hume, 1973). There was also a similar ability to broadly categorize stimuli between schizophrenics and creative individuals. Prentky focused on the ability to control as differentiating between the divergent thinking of schizophrenics and the divergent thinking of scientists. This is consistent with the psychoanalytic concept of *regression in the service of the ego* (Kris, 1952). It is the controlled access to primitive content, and the ability to evaluate the quality of an idea that differentiates between the novel responses that emerge from an individual with a serious thought disorder and the novel responses that come from the creative person. However, Prentky (1989) had a valid point when he stated that "the existence of such cognitive styles may facilitate creativity as well as reflect a genetic predisposition to psychosis" (p. 258). He concluded that creativity and the major mental illnesses are not causally related.

Martindale (1989) also wrestled with the relationship between creativity and mental illness. He pointed out that there is evidence that both the affective disorders and the thought disorders are more prevalent in creative individuals, yet the two disorders are not determined by the same gene. What the two illnesses have in common is access to primary process thought and disinhibition. He proposed a common trait of disinhibition. He viewed cognitive disinhibition as leading to behavioral disinhibition. However, this conceptualization does not fit with the concept of a controlled regression. Cognitive disinhibition, in well-adjusted individuals, would not lead to behavioral disinhibition.

Anne Sexton is an excellent example of a poet who had access to primitive material and who had a flow of associations, which she then channeled into poetry. This flow of associations, fluidity of thinking, and access to primary process material is evident throughout Middlebrook's recent biography of Sexton (1991). Clearly, Sexton had difficulty keeping control of her thoughts. The adaptive control necessary for "regression in the service of the ego" was not always present for her. However, she described how the creative process helped her to gain better control of her thoughts. This is an interesting reversal of how we usually view the creative process – that is, that the control comes first. Sexton said "It is the split self, it seems to me, that is the mad woman. When writing you make a new reality and become whole (. . . .). It is like lying on the analyst's couch, reenacting a private terror, and the creative mind is the analyst who gives pattern and meaning to what the persona sees as the only incoherent experience," (Middlebrook, 1991, p. 64). As Middlebrook pointed out, the therapist here has been internalized as a part of the creative mind. As one reads the examples in this book, it is evident that Sexton used the process of writing poetry to cognitively master difficult material, as the child uses play to cognitively integrate conflicts and stresses.

My own conclusion about the question of adjustment and creativity is that there are many routes to creativity. If the key ingredients involved in creativity are openness to affect-laden thoughts and affect states, openness to experience, divergent thinking, and a mix of various personality traits, then there are different routes to developing these processes. Several routes may interact in the same individual. One route may be a genetic predisposition to a serious mental illness. If so, one would expect creative productions to be episodic for those individuals and to occur when they were in a better functioning state. Another route to creativity is through good use of play and fantasy and the fostering of good emotional development. For adults, psychotherapy may help loosen free associations and help the individual to do creative work. For many creative individuals, an apt description is probably — open, sensitive, being in touch with affect and primary process themes (painful and pleasant), and basically adaptive and well-functioning.

ARTISTIC VERSUS SCIENTIFIC CREATIVITY

The personality differences between creative artists and creative scientists may reflect the differences in the domains of creativity and the cognitive and affective processes that are involved. Divergent thinking is important in scientific problem solving as well as artistic production. Breaking out of a set and creating new configurations is also important in both types of creativity. Kuhn's (1962) concept of revolution in science involved the overthrowing of a paradigm. This overthrowing of a paradigm involves a major breaking out of an old set. Clement (1989) had an excellent discussion of scientific reasoning where he described the importance of generating hypotheses and of breaking out of old sets for creative problem solving to occur. Feist (1991) found that at some times, forms of thinking for art students and science students are similar.

One of the main differences between artistic and scientific creativity may be the importance of getting more deeply into affect states and thematic material in artistic creativity. This in-depth involvement in the affective processes themselves may not be so necessary in scientific problem solving. Suler (1980) made a similar point. He reviewed work by Niederland (1973, 1976) that showed that artists incorporated early traumas and conflicts into their artistic products. Many scientists do not need to face into and incorporate affect-laden material into their scientific problem solving. For the scientist, good divergent thinking ability, transformation ability, and a flexible cognitive style may be sufficient for creative work to occur. For the writer or the musician or the artist, the need to get to basic affective content, primary process material, or drive-laden material may be necessary in order to be able to get to the universal truths that transcend the individual. The author David Gates described this process well. While describing the process of writing his latest novel, he said:

> I think what I wanted to do was to push all my worst imaginings and all my worst qualities to a terrible extreme and see what came of it. The isolation, the selfishness, the callousness, the indifference, the cruelty. Those awful qualities that are innate in all of us. I'm not uniquely that way. (Rothstein, 1991, p. B2)

You often hear artists and writers describe the need to get to this kind of experience. One can see how the need to live in that emotional state and to control that process may at times be disruptive, result in emotional instability and — some personal agony. Rothenberg (1990) described the anxiety that uncovering primary process material often creates in writers. He described the use of alcohol by so many writers to contain the anxiety. The movie *Naked Lunch* vividly portrays the agony of a writer facing uncontrolled bursts of primary process thinking and his struggle to transform that thinking into creative work.

One would assume that under optimal environmental conditions, the creative process for artists would be the same for men and for women. However, there are still a number of cultural taboos for women that might explain some of the gender differences that we find in the research literature. It may also help explain the lack of women on the lists of eminent writers, artists, musicians, and so on. It is still not as permissible for women to "explore the depths" either as children in play or as adults. Women have to work against the cultural pressures. Therefore, they would be at a disadvantage in the arts if they could not have as much access to this primitive material.

Virginia Woolf (Banks, 1920/1989) articulated possible reasons for gender differences. She wrote:

> It seems to me indisputable that the conditions which make it possible for a Shakespeare to exist are that he shall have had predecessors in his art, shall make one of a group where art is freely discussed and practiced, and shall himself have the utmost of freedom of action and experience. Perhaps in Lesbos, but never since, have these conditions been the lot of women. . . . But it is not education only that is needed. It is that women should have liberty of experience; that they should differ from men without fear and express their difference openly . . . that all activity of the mind should be so encouraged that there will always be in existence a nucleus of women who think, invent, imagine, and create as freely as men do, and with as little fear of ridicule and condescension (reprinted in New York Times, 1991)

Passion and Creativity

This brings us to the concept of passion and creativity. Passion is a major affective ingredient in the creative processes for both artists and scientists. Shaw (1989, in press) interviewed 14 scientists and engineers about the role of emotions in creative problem solving. The exhilaration and intense affect that accompanied discovery was a common theme. Stephanie Dudek has spoken about the importance of passion and creativity. Her long-term follow-up study of MacKinnon's architects and artists found that passionate commitment and involvement in their work is a quality found in many of these individuals (1991). Roe (1952) spoke of the driving absorption in work of her eminent scientists. The concept of passion was a characteristic mentioned by Anastasi and Schaefer (1969) in their study of creative adolescent girls. Passionate involvement in an area was one of the qualities of these creative girls. Torrance (1988) stressed the importance of love of the area in creative children. Having a career image they could stick with was a predictor for children of adult creative achievement. Torrance reached the conclusion that "the essence of the creative person is being in love with what one is doing" (p. 68). The title of his 1987 book *The Blazing Drive* reflects this quality. Csikszentmihalyi (1990) spoke of the exhilarating pleasure of mental activity. He quoted the Nobel-prize winning Michelson who replied when asked why he studied the velocity of light that "it was so much fun."

Passion can be at a rather primitive, sensual, raw level in the individual. John Updike (1989) had a good description in his recent book, *Self Consciousness,* of the early primitive passion that he can recall when he first began working with letters and blocks. This is a good description of the early primitive libidinal investment that may be an underpinning of creative work for many artists:

Alphabetical symbols stamped on blocks marked the dawn of my consciousness, along with the smell of oilcloth, the extra-fuzzy texture of the rug underneath the dining-room table, the eerie flexibility of my own hands, and the shine on other people's shoes. My early toys, kept in an old-fashioned country bushel basket, included three kinds of blocks: big, elemental ABC's, enamelled the colors of the rainbow and holding their letters in sans-serif intaglio that a finger and a wobbly crayon could trace; small blocks of a more intricate texture, with a serifed alphabet and primal objects like apples and bananas and railroad cabooses lifted in bas-relief from a flatness hollowed between rims that were in turn lightly incised; and a medium sized set featuring along with the numbers and letters, Walt Disney characters from Mickey Mouse to Horace Horsecollar. The second set, put in the mouth, tasted of wood, and was painted only on the raised parts, much as type is inked. What early intimations of the printing process tumbled in on me with my manipulations, my assembly and disassembly, of that bushel basket full of blocks, I can only retrospectively guess at; but I still carry intact within me my happiness when, elevated by the thickness of some books to the level of my mother's typewriter, I began to tap the keyboard and saw the perfect letter-forms leap up on the paper rolled around the platen. (p. 104)

The concept of passion is important because it speaks to the importance of the creative individual's ability to tolerate affect, pleasant as well as unpleasant. In the case of passion, it is tolerance for and, perhaps, desire of extreme pleasure that is important.

In conclusion, the personality trait approach to studying creativity has been a rather global approach. It has resulted in some consensus about personality characteristics of creative individuals. On the other hand, more could be done to focus the research on specific cognitive and affective mechanisms involved in creativity.

Most researchers agree that no one cognitive, affective, or personality trait is sufficient to ensure that a creative product will emerge and that there is no fixed formula for predicting creativity. The approach to creativity that Sternberg and Lybart (1991) used in their investment theory of creativity is a good one. They envisioned creativity as stemming from a confluence of resources, with differential contributions across different domains. Many resources must converge in order to generate a truly creative product.

6

Mood-Induction and Motivational Systems Approaches to Creativity

Another major set of research programs has looked at the role of a specific affective process or of motivational systems in creativity. This chapter reviews the mood-induction research, intrinsic motivation, and curiosity.

MOOD-INDUCTION

The work on mood-induction and creativity is an important area of research. The mood-induction paradigm provides a way of altering affect states (and perhaps affect-laden thoughts) so that the effect on cognitive processes can be observed. The mood-induction paradigm was reviewed in chapter 3. This procedure can be used with adults or children. For children, as developed by Mischel et al. (1972), children are asked to think affectively valenced thoughts, that is, "think about something that's fun." Children think about an experience that is associated with a particular emotion. Affect can also be induced in other ways such as by giving gifts or showing films, in both children and adults. Manipulation checks of the affect induced have been carried out by observers' ratings of facial expression, subject ratings of the pleasantness of unfamiliar words (Isen et al., 1987), and self-reports of feeling states (Jausovec, 1989).

Alice Isen has done very important work on the effect of affective states on creative thinking. In a series of studies, she found that induced positive affect facilitated creative thinking. In a study by Isen and Daubman (1984), adults in the positive affect condition categorized stimuli more inclusively than controls. On a sorting task, more items were seen as related. Isen hypothesized that positive affect may influence how cognitive material is organized and therefore influence creativity.

In a 1985 study, Isen found that the positive affect condition resulted in more divergent associations to neutral words.

In a set of studies in 1987, Isen et al. found that positive affect, induced by a comedy film, resulted in more creative problem solving than control conditions. The problem-solving task in one study was the Duncker (1945) candle task, which is a measure of functional fixedness. To solve the problem, one must break a set and consider alternative solutions to the problem. This problem seems quite similar to the Luchins' Water-Jar Test used in Russ' (1982) study discussed in chapter 2. In Russ' study, for boys, access to primary process material was related to the ability to break set in two separate samples. Positive results for girls occurred in one of the samples. Both the Duncker candle task and the Luchins' Water-Jar Task are measures of Guilford's transformation ability.

Isen et al. also found that positive affect improved performance on the remote associates test, a measure of creativity that calls for diverse associations and seeing relatedness of ideas. Isen concluded that the underlying mechanism for these results is that positive affect cues positive memories and a large amount of cognitive material. This process results in defocused attention and a more complex cognitive context. This, in turn, results in a greater range of associations and interpretations. Also, there is an increasing awareness of different aspects of stimuli and more ways of relating and combining information.

Isen et al. (1987) also induced a negative affect state, using a film, and found no effect on problem solving. They cautioned against overinterpreting the lack of results with the negative affect condition. The film was an extremely negative one of the Holocaust that may have resulted in a major inhibition in the viewers.

Actually, Isen's hypothesis of cued memories occurring in the induced affective state should hold for negative affect as well as positive affect if the negative state is not so extreme as to overwhelm the subject.

Isen's work is important because it clearly demonstrates that induced positive affect states facilitate cognitive processes that are important in creativity. Her research design was of high quality with reasonable control conditions. (For example, one of her control conditions ruled out high arousal as a possible explanation of the results). She used both male and female subjects and, apparently, there were no gender differences. This work gives support to the correlational studies in the affect and creativity area whose patterns of results suggest a causal relationship between affect and creativity, but can go no further.

Jausovec (1989) also found that induced positive affect facilitated performance on a cognitive task. Induced positive affect (using a film) facilitated analogical transfer in ill-defined problems. Analogical transfer is thought to be important in creative thinking (Sternberg, 1988) and ill-defined problems are those that have a number of different possible solutions. Jausovec also found that positive affect impaired performance on a logical problem-solving task. His conclusion from these studies was that affect influences the way in which material is processed. Positive affect facilitates the use of analogy in insight. It does this by creating a more complex cognitive context. More associations are available that increase the likelihood that a "pointer" in memory will trigger the analogy. Positive affect interferes with logical problem solving because the increased complexity of the cognitive context brought about by the affect state increases the amount of information in the system. An increase in information can impair performance in well-defined logical problem-solving tasks (Julisch & Krause, 1976). Jausovec also looked at the effect of negative affect on problem solving and found no effect. However, as Isen did, Jausovec used a very negative Holocaust film.

It is interesting to compare Isen's explanation of her results with the psychoanalytic explanation of the relationship between primary processes and creativity. Psychoanalytic theory also focuses on increased associations because of lack of repression or blockage of ideas, memories, and associations. The focus is not on memories per se. However, Isen's explanation is compatible with psychoanalytic theory. Those individuals who have better access to affect-laden thematic material and are comfortable with this material may have a broader range of memories and associations available to them. In addition, they may be more likely to permit affective states to occur and to be responsive to affect arousing stimuli. They may naturally do what Isen induced. Thus, in the incubation stage of the creative process, there would be more likelihood that these individuals would let these affective processes occur, which in turn would effect cognition. It would be interesting to see if access to affective material would function as a moderator variable in Isen's studies. That is, would the mood-induction be more effective for individuals who already had good access to affect-laden content?

Isen's early work with Shalker, Clark, and Karp (1978) looked at affect and memory. They found that words consistent in valence with the subject's emotional state were recalled more frequently than inconsistent words.

Isen's findings are consistent with the work of Bower (1981) on mood-linked state dependent learning mechanisms and with Rholes et al. (1987). Bower concluded from his work that encoding for memory storage is partly determined by mood state at the time of encoding. Rholes et al. (1987) found that positive memories were more quickly recalled after positive mood-induction, and negative memories more quickly recalled after negative mood-induction. They hypothesized a cognitive priming process where mood states resulted in mood relevant cognitions that can cue other memories.

In the area of creativity, the individual who is open to affect-laden material would have the advantage because more memories and other kinds of cognitions would be cued and available for use. More associations could occur. Primary process thinking could be conceptualized as mood-relevant cognitions, which then cue other memories. Because primary process material is content around which the child experienced early, intense emotions, access to this content could tap into a wide range of memories and associations.

The effect of negative affect on creativity needs to be thoroughly explored. Some theories would suggest that negative and positive affect should be equally facilitative of creativity. The mechanisms should be similar. However, the empirical results are mixed. Masters et al. (1979) found that mood-induction of a negative mood state retarded learning in children. Easterbrook (1959) found that negative affect resulted in constriction of thinking and a decrease in cue utilization. Isen found no effect, although she cautions that her film was extremely negative. On the other hand, in my work on children's fantasy and play, which found that affect in fantasy did relate to creativity, many of the play themes were negative, with a high proportion of themes in the aggressive affect category. In a recent master's thesis by Adaman (1991), negative mood-induction did result in increased performance on a divergent thinking test in college students. Mood was induced using musical mood-induction tapes. Positive mood-induction also increased divergent thinking when compared to a neutral condition. There needs to be further empirical investigation of this issue. Perhaps what will emerge is a curvilinear relationship between negative affect and creativity. Negative affect may facilitate creativity when it is of low to moderate levels. At those levels, such as in fantasy (in the Rorschach) or in well-controlled play, where the child is in charge of the pacing of the material, negative affect may indeed trigger memories and associations important to the creative process. Because the child is in charge of the material in good pretend play, negative affect may not be so negative. As Singer and Singer (1990) have said, controlled expression of negative affect is reinforcing. In more intense negative affect states, such as some of the mood-induction work, other factors, such as constriction of cue utilization, may begin to take over. Similar to the work on anxiety and problem solving, moderate amounts of negative affect, especially in the form of affect themes, may be facilitative, whereas high levels of negative affect states may inhibit creativity. This type of curvilinear relationship has been found by Toplyn and Maguire (1991) for creativity under different levels of noise conditions for highly original subjects. Gender differences may operate here as well, and need to be explored. The interaction between gender and specific affective processes may be an important factor. Certainly, there is more evidence that access to negative affect relates to creativity in males than in females. The use of different research paradigms to assess negative affect will be useful. Affect in play and the Rorschach may reflect affect themes and mild affect states whereas mood-induction may arouse more intense affect states.

The play situation may be a very important one in developing modes of expression of affective material. In this safe arena, children can call up a variety of mood states, memories and fantasies, and primary process material. Negative affect can be expressed, worked through, and mastered. Children can practice with free association and divergent thinking. Over time, this practice could alter structures and result in better divergent thinking. This kind of speculation was put forth by Pine and Holt in 1960, when they talked about a different kind of cognitive style developing for individuals who integrated primary process well.

Studies investigating mood-induction in children and the effect on creativity tasks need to be carried out. Work is being done on this question in Isen's lab. Also, one of my students, Hilary Katz, is investigating the effect of positive and negative mood-induction on divergent thinking in second- and third-grade children. She is using amount of affective expression in play as a moderator variable.

Greene and Noice (1988) reported that induced positive affect in eighth-grade children facilitates solving the Dunker Candle Task, generating examples of categories of a word, and generating unusual examples of words.

In the adult area, we can conclude that careful experimental work shows that some positive affect states facilitate transformation abilities, remote associations, and analogical transfer. Future work needs to explore the effect of specific positive affect states and mild specific negative affect states on creative cognitive processes.

MOTIVATIONAL SYSTEMS

The whole area of motivation subsumes needs, drives, and affective processes. Drive refers to both primary and acquired drives. Two major motivational systems found to be important to creativity and that include affective components are intrinsic motivation and curiosity.

Intrinsic Motivation

Amabile (1983, 1990b) has a major research program in the area of intrinsic motivation. Amabile continued the work of MacKinnon (1965) and Barron (1969) on intrinsic motivation. Her model of creativity presents three basic components (1983). Domain-relevant skills include abilities, talents, and knowledge specific to a specific area. Creativity-relevant skills include cognitive and personality characteristics traditionally associated with creativity. Affective processes would come under this category. Amabile does touch on the importance of affect and is beginning to carry out research investigating mood-induction in her laboratory (1990a).

The third component of Amabile's model is task motivation, which is where the bulk of her research program has focused. Looking at intrinsic versus extrinsic motivation and creativity, in a series of studies, Amabile found repeated evidence that intrinsic motivation, that is, the motivation that has to do with "the intrinsic value in the attaining of the creative solution itself" (Crutchfield, 1962, p. 121, quoted by Amabile, 1983), is conducive to creativity. She stated that the evidence is so strong that she now refers to the intrinsic motivation principle of creativity (1990b). Her conclusions from studies with both children and adults are that expected evaluation, being watched, contracted for reward, competition, and restricted choice in how to do an activity all have detrimental effects on creativity. All of these conditions are forms of extrinsic motivation. In general, extrinsic motivation negatively affect intrinsic motivation, which in turn inhibits creativity.

Amabile stated that intrinsic motivation is certainly important for task persistence and seeing a project through. Intrinsic motivation also affects creativity directly by ensuring exploration of solutions. As Amabile (1990b) put it:

> Finding a creative solution requires exploration through the maze, a more heuristic approach to the task. Individuals will only be likely to take this more creative approach if they are initially intrinsically interested in the activity itself and if their social environment does not demand a narrowing of behavior into the familiar algorithm. (p. 86)

Intrinsic motivation is also accompanied by positive affect. Amabile (1990b) credited Csikszentmihalyi (1975) and Izard (1977) for hypothesizing about this particular association. Certainly, the deep pleasure taken in the creative act can be viewed as a positive affective experience. Csikszentmihalyi (1990a) described the deep pleasure taken in creative tasks.

My own view of the component of intrinsic motivation is that it is terribly important in task persistence and task involvement. It may set the stage for the individual to be able to utilize their creative abilities in a particular area. And the positive affect link may facilitate specific cognitive abilities. However, intrinsic motivation per se is not a major component in the specific cognitive abilities such as divergent thinking and transformation abilities important to creativity. Intrinsic motivation sets the stage for the related affective processes to occur.

Curiosity

Spielberger, Peters, and Frain (1981) and Spielberger and Starr (in press) summarized the various theoretical approaches to curiosity. Curiosity has long been thought to be important in creative behavior. William James (1890) viewed curiosity as being instinctive. Freud also thought of curiosity as a biological drive and also as a method for reducing feelings of insecurity. Spielberger et al. had a thorough review of Berlyne's (1966) work on curiosity. Berlyne viewed curiosity as reflecting the organism's striving to maintain an optimal level of arousal.

Spielberger et al. (1981) put forth an optimal stimulation/dual process theory of exploratory behavior that takes both anxiety and curiosity into account. Their approach proposes seven basic principles:

1. The curiosity drive is conceptualized as motivating stimulus-seeking, that is, exploratory behavior designed to increase arousal. The arousal threshold for the curiosity drive (Berlyne's reward system) is lower (closer to zero stimulus intensity) than for the anxiety drive (Berlyne's aversion system).

2. The anxiety drive is conceptualized as motivating stimulus avoidance, that is, behavior that reduces stimulus intensity or arousal potential. The asymptotic level of the anxiety drive is greater than that of the curiosity drive.

3. Subjective feelings of pleasantness are associated with the growth of the curiosity drive as a function of increasing stimulus intensity and arousal of the positive reward system.

4. Subjective feelings of unpleasantness are associated with the growth of the anxiety drive as a function of increasing stimulus intensity and arousal associated with increasing activity of the aversion system.

5. The combination of differential thresholds, different growth rates, and different asymptotic levels for the curiosity and anxiety drives produce a resultant curve that closely approximates Wundt's curve for hedonic tone. With increasing stimulus intensity (arousal), subjective experiences increase in pleasantness up to an optimal level, then decrease to a point of indifference, and finally become increasingly unpleasant.

6. The "point of indifference" that is reached at a moderately high level of arousal reflects a relatively intense conflict between a near-asymptotic curiosity drive that strongly stimulates exploratory behavior, and a substantially elevated level of state anxiety that motivates avoidance behavior.

7. At low levels of collative stimulus intensity, curiosity and diversive exploration will predominate. At moderate collative stimulus intensity, the combination of high curiosity and moderate anxiety will motivate specific exploration. With high collative stimulus intensity, high anxiety will motivate avoidance behavior.

Spielberger stressed the need for empirical research in this area to specify the parameters of anxiety and curiosity. Spielberger's State-Trait Curiosity Inventory is one measure that will help explore these empirical links.

Curiosity, in general, is important to creativity because interest in novelty and exploration aids in problem identification as well as task persistence. Curiosity serves as an important motivator for creative acts. It might be a reflection of intrinsic motivation or vice versa. Also, the highly curious and risk-taking individual is more likely to gain a wide variety of experience that would add to their knowledge base.

In conclusion, the research programs in the areas of mood-induction, intrinsic motivation, and curiosity are shedding light on the role of affect in the creative process. The research paradigms employed in these studies have been fruitful and should continue to be applied in future work.

7 Neurological Processes, Artificial Intelligence, and Creativity

Neurological underpinnings of creativity and artificial intelligence need to be discussed with a focus on affect and cognition. The purpose of this chapter is to give a broad outline of what we currently know in these fields and to explain how this relates to the role of affect in creative thinking. This chapter is not a thorough or sophisticated review of the literature, because this is not my area of expertise. However, there is current work that is contributing to a growing understanding of cognitive-affective interactions in creative thinking. I attempt to highlight the major threads and the implications for creativity.

The work on mood and memory suggest that the search process for associations is broadened by the involvement of emotion. This broadened search process would facilitate creative cognitive processes such as divergent thinking, transformation abilities, and analogical transfer. The role of primary process thinking might be better understood if it is conceptualized as mood-relevant cognition. When stirred, it triggers a broad associative network. As the role of affect in the creative process gains increasing importance, one must look anew at the artificial intelligence area. Can computers simulate creative problem solving if affect influences cognitive functioning?

This chapter discusses the work on mood and memory and its implications for the role of affect and primary process thinking; neurological correlates of creativity, and artificial intelligence and creativity.

AFFECT AND COGNITION

Bower (1981), in his classic article "Mood and Memory," reviewed a series of studies and presented a theoretical framework of affect and memory processes. Bower induced happy and sad moods in adults by hypnotic suggestion. Subjects demonstrated a greater percentage of recall of those experiences that were affectively congruent with the mood during recall. Subjects in an induced pleasant mood state recalled a greater percentage of recent pleasant life experiences than of unpleasant life experiences. The opposite effect occurred for the unpleasant mood states. The same effect held for childhood memories. Emotions also influenced free associations and imaginative fantasies. These results reflected two basic phenomena:

1. mood congruity effect — people attend to and learn more about events that match their emotional state
2. mood state dependent retention — if, during recall, the original emotional state when the material was originally learned is reinstated, then recall is better.

Bower proposed the associative network theory to explain these phenomena. Each emotion is a memory unit — each emotion has a special node or unit in memory. The activation of the emotion unit aids the retrieval of events associated with it. It primes emotional themata for use in free association, fantasies, and perceptual categorization. Each emotion node includes autonomic reactions, expressive behavior, descriptions, and verbal labels. When activated, it spreads activation through memory structures. Therefore, if material was learned in a specific affect state, search cues are activated in memory when that affect state occurs. This effect is most evident in the free recall condition.

In the encoding process itself, emotion should effect the salience of mood congruent material for selective attention and learning. The associative links would be stronger for mood-congruent events. The emotional response is part of the associative network. Bower's theory is applicable to the area of creativity in that the search process is broadened by the involvement of emotion. A broad search process would aid divergent thinking and transformation abilities. This point was the basis of Mednick's (1962) associationistic theory of creativity. The ability to make remote associations increases with a relatively flat, broad gradient of the associative hierarchy.

Since 1981, a number of studies have empirically supported Bower's theory and empirical results. Rholes et al. (1987) had a good review of these studies. For example, Clark and Teasdale (1982) demonstrated that in naturally occurring depression, there was an increase in access to memories of affectively consistent life experiences. Rholes et al. (1987) expanded on Bower's theory and discussed mood-related cognitions. Affect states activate a set of relevant cognitions that are other memories. Affect stirs mood-related cognitions. A cognitive priming process occurs. Both positive and negative affect states show activation of mood-relevant cognition. Natale and Hanlas (1982) found that induced depression caused a decrease in recall of pleasant life experiences and tended to recall more unpleasant life experiences. However, as Rholes et al. (1987) concluded, positive mood induction has stronger effects on memory than negative mood induction. They speculated that it may be harder in general to gain access to negative content.

Lazarus took a comprehensive view of emotion and cognition in his recent book *Emotion & Adaptation* (1991). He viewed emotion as being inseparable from cognition and motivation. These are complex, interrelated process. He stated that "emotions are, in effect, organized cognitive–motivational–relational configurations whose status changes with changes in the person–environment relationship as this is perceived and evaluated (appraised)" (p. 38). Cognitive appraisal, both conscious and unconscious, is necessary in determining emotions. Lazarus offered a thorough review of theories of emotion and emotional development. He took a rather extreme position by viewing emotion as always involving cognition—personal meaning of some sort. He stressed that a comprehensive, global approach is crucial in understanding emotion and cognitive interaction. (This is at odds with more specific research approaches taken by Isen et al., 1987; Jausevec, 1989; and Russ, 1987.)

Zajonc (1980, 1990) had a different view of affect and cognition. Zajonc posited that affect and cognition are two separate processes. Affective reactions can occur without prior involvement of cognitive processes. Cognition and affect are two interacting but independent functions. Also, some stimuli pull for affective responses without cognitive involvement.

Zajonc's work is consistent with recent work by LeDoux. In research with rats, LeDoux (1989) found that the amygdala triggers an emotional reaction before the thinking brain has fully processed the nerve signals. The amygdala can receive inputs from the senses before going through the cortex. LeDoux referred to the existence of emotional memories. The emotional system can act independently of the cognitive system. His work has discovered neural pathways that do not go through the cortex. LeDoux suggested that these precognitive emotions are functional in infants, during the early formative years. Behavior is effected, but we have no conscious memory of the events.

NEUROLOGICAL CORRELATES OF CREATIVE THOUGHT

With the development of the CAT-scan and PET scanner technology, we can map cerebral activity and obtain a picture of brain involvement during problem solving. Eventually, we should learn about the actual neurological processes involved in creative problem solving. To date, there has been some beginning work in the area of creativity.

A study by Hudspith (1985) shows differences in brain wave activity between high creatives and low creatives, based on creativity tests. High creatives during association tasks, showed lower visual cortex and higher prefrontal amplitudes.

Martindale (1989) theorized that creative individuals are more prone to states of defocused attention. This idea was first put forth by Mendelshohn (1976). Defocused attention is more likely to occur during low cortical arousal. In this state, a large number of nodes (neurons or groups of neurons) are activated simultaneously. As Martindale put it, the more nodes and relationships that are activated at a given time, the greater the likelihood that an analogy will be noticed between two different elements. There is evidence that primary process thinking involves defocused attention and low cortical arousal (Martindale, 1981). More creative individuals showed lower levels of cortical arousal while performing creative tasks (Martindale & Hines, 1975). Lower levels of cortical arousal occurred during the inspiration stage than during the elaboration stage (Martindale & Hasenfus, 1978). However, Martindale pointed out that creative individuals are not in a state of low physiological arousal. In fact, they showed higher levels of basal arousal on physiological measures (Martindale, 1990). Martindale concluded that creative individuals may be more variable in their level of arousal than uncreative people. He pointed out that this is really similar to Kris' (1952) concept of creative individuals being more able to regress in the service of the ego, thus showing more variability on the primary process–secondary process continuum.

PRIMARY PROCESS, AFFECT, NEUROLOGICAL PROCESSES, AND CREATIVITY

The theoretical approaches of Bower and Martindale both may be useful in understanding the facilitative role of affect on creativity and the role of primary process thinking. These approaches are not necessarily contradictory. Both may be operative in the creative process.

Looking first at Bower's associative network theory, individuals who are open to affect states and to affect-laden cognition may benefit in carrying out creative tasks in two ways. First, they have access to more cues that activate other nodes in the search process. Isen et al. (1987) explained their findings that positive affect induction facilitated creativity on the basis of Bower's theory. Positive affect cued positive memories, thus resulting in a more complex context. More associations occurred and there was a defocusing of attention. In essence, individuals who are more open to affect would activate more emotion nodes and emotion relevant associations. This aids the divergent thinking process by increasing the number of associations available. It would also aid the ability to shift sets, see new solutions to problems, and develop new insights.

Primary process thinking itself might be conceptualized as mood-relevant cognition. Primary process thoughts may occur when emotion nodes are activated. Perhaps there is a fusing of emotion and cognition in many primary process thoughts. If, as Russ proposed (1987), primary process is a subtype of affect in cognition that consists of content around which the child had experienced early intense feeling states (oral, anal, aggressive), then current primary process expressions could reflect these early encodings of fused affect and cognition. The primary process content was stored when emotion was present. Access to this primary process material would activate emotion nodes and associations, thus broadening the search process.

A second way that access to affect states and affect-laden cognition would aid creativity, if we apply Bower's theory, is that more emotionally salient material would get coded and stored when individuals were in an emotional state. For individuals open to affect, more would "get in," thus providing the individual with a richer network of affect relevant associations. This storing of affective content would be especially important for artistic creativity, where one is often dealing with affect and the transformation of affect content into universal symbols. Indeed, there is evidence that creative individuals are more sensitive and open to experience (McCrae & Costa, 1987; Richards, 1990) than noncreative people.

Bower's theory does not explain all aspects of affect and creativity. The improved search process due to more cues and associations available is not sufficient to explain all the phenomena that we observe in creative thinking. Martindale's view of low cortical arousal and defocused attention hypothesizes the existence of a different process that also aids in creativity. It is possible that individuals who are comfortable with affect and primary process thinking let these low cortical arousal states occur, because they are comfortable with the results. This is what Kris (1952) was saying with his concept of "regression in the service of ego." Individuals who can gain access to primary process in a controlled fashion are more likely to let this state occur.

It would be interesting to carry out studies that would integrate Bower's theory and Martindale's theory. Low levels of cortical arousal might enhance the phenomena of the mood congruity effect and the mood state dependent retention. Taking a different view, low levels of arousal may enhance creativity more in those individuals who are open to affect than for those who are not. Thus, there may be differential effects for open to affect and closed to affect groups.

A word about children's play. As we have said before, in play children practice with expressing affect and primary process material. They get comfortable with it. This should help them in their daily life to stay open to affect states and affect arousing stimuli. They become more likely to let natural mood states occur. This openness to affect should effect the process of storage of material in memory, retention of and access to those memories, and the likelihood that they would let themselves enter situations that are conducive to low arousal states as they get older.

Finally, in thinking about primary process, one thinks of the preverbal origins of this thinking and the importance of images in primary process. Recently, work by Marcus Raichle with the PET scanner showed that the visual processing area is involved in some memory tasks (Begley, 1991). They found that a number of different areas of the brain are involved in memory tasks. We might speculate that access to primary process preverbal images somehow aids search strategies in creative thinking. Einstein spoke of the importance of images in his thinking process:

> The words or the language, as they are written or spoken, do not seem to play any role in any mechanism of thought. The psychical entities which seem to serve as elements of thought are certain signs and more or less clear images which can be "voluntarily" reproduced and combined. The above mentioned elements are, in my case, of visual and some muscular type. Conventional words or other signs have to be sought for laboriously only in a second stage, when the mentioned associative play is sufficiently established and can be reproduced at will. (Penrose, 1989, p. 423)

ARTIFICIAL INTELLIGENCE

Penrose (1989) tackled the difficult question of "can the computer have a mind?" in his recent book *The Emperor's New Mind*. It has long been debated as to whether or not the computer will eventually be able to simulate all functions of the brain. Penrose took the position that it will not. He gave a thorough review of the debates in the world of artificial intelligence.

The strong artificial intelligence (AI) group proposes that all brain processes can be simulated—it is just a matter of time. If we can figure out the correct algorithms and formulas, the computer could have a mind equal to that of a person. The logical structure of the algorithms that would spell out all the rules of problem solving and information processing need to be developed. Simon (1985) conceptualized creative problem solving as involving normal problem-solving operations. In George Johnson's (1990) review of Penrose's book, Johnson concluded that the "computer metaphor is broad and flexible enough to accommodate a theory of the mind" (p.49). He conceptualized the brain as a computer—and the mind is software running on this neurological machine. Langley and Jones (1988) held that cognitive processes involved in creative thinking can be simulated. Their theory of scientific insight is based on a spreading activation theory that triggers stored structures. Insight involves the recognition, evaluation, and the elaboration of analogies. These processes, once the details are spelled out, should be subject to computer simulation.

Penrose, on the other hand, concluded that something other than logical processes are frequently involved and the brain must be doing something "nonalgorithmic." He discussed concepts of consciousness and judgement as ones that are difficult for current computer models to encompass. He concluded that computers are superior in tasks requiring quick calculations whereas people are better at tasks that require time and judgement. Penrose proposed that the principle of quantum theory may be important in brain functioning. The idea that the brain is processing a number of simultaneous possibilities that are somehow combined into a good configuration might be better explained by quantum theory than by the logic of the algorithmic script. Krystal and Krystal (in press) also stressed the importance of a nonlinear model of brain functioning in creative thought.

Consciousness is often presented as the stumbling block for computers. How is the concept of consciousness explained in artificial intelligence? Artificial intelligence may also lack problem-finding ability, a point made by Csikszentmihalyi (1988). Simon (1988) refuted this claim and considers problem-finding ability as a normal problem-solving process. It seems to me, however, in reviewing the literature, that affect is the real stumbling block for the computer metaphor. Because affect is often not recognized as a process that can actually influence and interact with cognitive processes, it has gone largely unrecognized as an important concept in the world of artificial intelligence. If, as the growing evidence suggests, affect is especially important in creative thinking, then the computer metaphor would be particularly weak in encompassing creativity. Penrose concluded that it is weak, although he does not address the "affect" issue. Csikszentmihalyi (1988) stressed the need for integrating affect and motivation into our view of what thought consists of.

If we think this issue through, the important question is whether the role of affect and drive in creative thinking can be simulated in the computer. Can we somehow build it in? The strong AI people would say that, once we identify the rules and principles involved, we will be able to simulate the interactions between affect and cognition. Penrose even suggested that we could devise pleasure and pain scores with directives for behavior and decision making—although he raises the question as to whether this would truly be affect.

As we have thought about affect throughout this book, affect would be involved in creative problem solving in several different ways. First, access to affect content and affect states increases divergent thinking and random search activities. This is probably the easiest area for the computer to handle. Increasing random search activities and flicking on a whole area of associations when an affect content theme is activated should be able to be simulated. Of course, what is unique about each individual is the particular idiosyncratic range of associations that gets triggered by specific affect content because each individual has a different experience.

Another way we have said that affect alters cognition is in determining the actual creative product itself. That is, especially for the artist, affect content itself is utilized to come up with a universal symbol or universal truth that captures universal experience. The individual digs deeply within and transforms the particular into the universal. This transformation process is dependent on the affective experience. It is doubtful whether this transforming process could be truly simulated by the computer. This controlled fusion and condensation we so often see in dreams and fantasy (and on the Rorschach) of primary process material, which is so often "the stuff of which art is made," would be difficult to simulate because the processing rules are, by definition, alogical. Primary process thought is by definition, alogical thought. Primary process utilizes images and nonverbal processing. Penrose accurately pointed out that much creative thinking is nonverbal and is in the form of images. He was speaking specifically about the realm of mathematics, but it is true of many other disciplines as well.

A third way affect is important in creativity is its role in the positive enjoyment of the creative act. Deep pleasure is taken in the creative process and creativity is intrinsically motivating (Amabile, 1983). Creativity feeds on itself, so to speak—one act leads to another in doing a large work or in developing a body of work, in art or science, over a period of time. This is Csikszentmihalyi's (1990a) concept of flow. The love of the work is mentioned by most creative individuals (MacKinnon, 1965) and creativity researchers as an important component.

Again, one could build in pleasure codes in the computer with directives to keep on going with the task, but one could certainly make the argument that something is missing that would weaken the creative product.

Finally, affect is important in recognizing both the problem to be worked on and the solution, when it finally comes. The tension, and perhaps, pleasurable anticipation of the challenge that comes when recognizing a problem, or sensing the ambiguity in a situation, helps the creative individual to see a problem where others have not. The affective experience serves as a cue. Simon (1985, 1988) spoke of the important element of surprise in scientific work in identifying problems. Can the affective component of surprise be simulated on the computer? Simon, of course, would say "yes." The pleasure that comes when the solution is found, or the composition is formulated, helps the creator know when to stop, or which of the myriad of ideas and configurations is correct. Again, the computer is at a great disadvantage without these affective cues. Penrose spoke of the role of recognizing universal truths in mathematical solutions. In this Platoneon view, the universal truths that are out there are to be seen and discovered. Complex judgement and aesthetic pleasure are involved in the recognition of optimal solutions. What is right "feels" right.

In the final analysis, we know that computers can simulate random search processes and formulate good solutions to problems. What remains to be seen is whether or not we can build-in a life history with affect-coded components. Can we build in a developmental history with oral, aggressive, and sexual associations, losses, deep pleasures, and mood-relevant memories that trigger other associations? If we can, will those affective experiences have the depth necessary to result in art that has universal symbolism or science that achieves universal truths? My guess is that we can not, but in trying to get there, we may learn more about the processes, rules, and laws that govern affective–cognitive interaction.

8 Implications for Home, Educational, and Therapeutic Environments

My interest in creativity and affect in children began in the early 1970s when I was working with a number of children in psychotherapy at Washington University Child Guidance Center. I noticed with many of these children, especially those who had no major developmental problems and were dealing with conflicts and anxiety, that as they become more open to affect they seemed to become more flexible thinkers, more creative, and more humorous. I noticed this phenomena with a number of children and, while at Case Western Reserve University, developed a research program to investigate the area. In therapy, children gain access to affect states and affect-laden thoughts through play and through verbalization. Of all the child specialists, therapists are probably the most skilled in facilitating access to affective material in children. We should listen to them and to the clinical literature in developing guidelines for parents and teachers about how to facilitate affect and fantasy in play.

I find myself to be quite ambivalent about including a section on enhancing creativity and creative development. I do not think there are any quick techniques that will increase true creativity. It is, however, worthwhile to develop principles for childrearing, school environments, work environments, and adult lifestyles that help individuals develop the abilities, over time, that will result in creative work. Much of what we can now say about developing creativity emerges from research projects designed to learn about personality, affect, and cognitive relationships, psychotherapy process and outcome research, and basic research and theory in child development.

ENHANCING AFFECTIVE EXPRESSION IN CHILDREN'S PLAY

Reisman (1973) developed some broad principles of psychotherapy that help to create an environment in which the child should feel freer to express emotions. He stressed that the therapist should listen to the child, allow opportunities for the expression of feelings and beliefs, and communicate understanding and respect for the child. It is important that the therapist create a safe and comfortable environment and accept the child's expressions (Axline, 1947; A. Freud, 1965). Axline (1947) especially emphasized the importance of a permissive environment. Labeling of affect is also helpful (Dorfman, 1951; Ginott, 1965). Giving the child verbal permission to express feelings in play is facilitative of affective expression in therapy. In most forms of child therapy, interpretation of the child's affect and play is an important part of the process. As children are freed-up and are able to resolve conflicts, they gain more access to affective material. I think that interpretation is the one technique that is not usually applicable to the home or school environment. Parents and teachers could facilitate play in a variety of ways, stopping short of interpretation. This should be enough to help most children to use play effectively. For those children with serious conflicts or developmental problems who can not use play adequately, then a therapist is the appropriate option.

Freedheim and Russ (1983, 1992) stressed that, in therapy, play occurs within the context of a trusting relationship. In this way, play in therapy is different from the natural play situation. In addition, the adult is making suggestions, labeling, guiding, and interpreting. The effective therapist follows the child's lead in determining the play content and in setting the pace of the play.

The principles that therapists use that could be used by parents and teachers to facilitate the expression of affect in play are:

1. Be accepting of the child's expression of feelings.
2. Give verbal permission for expression of feelings.
3. Create a permissive environment (but set limits when needed).
4. Develop a comfortable relationship with the child.
5. Label feelings that are expressed.
6. Listen to the child and empathize.
7. Enjoy the child's play and fantasy.
8. Have appropriate toys available — a variety and relatively unstructured.
9. Follow the child's lead in determining the play.

10. Depending on the child, stay uninvolved in the play itself. Only give the guidance that the child needs to get going, get unstuck, and feel comfortable.

Let us now look more specifically at the home environment.

THE HOME ENVIRONMENT

In *The House of Make-Believe* Singer and Singer (1990) stressed the importance of safety and acceptance in the home environment for enhancing play and fantasy. They specifically refer to a longitudinal study by Harrington, Block and Block (1987). This is a very important study and is worth discussing in some detail. Their study tests the principles put forth by Rogers (1954), who stated that creativity in children was most likely to occur when three conditions were present: openness to experience, internal locus of evaluation, and the ability to toy with elements and concepts. He stated that these three internal conditions were fostered by two external conditions — psychological safety and psychological freedom. These two external conditions are similar to those stressed by child therapists in fostering expression of affect and conflict resolution. Rogers felt that for safety to occur, people in the environment must accept the individual as having unconditional worth; must understand the individual empathically; and the environment must be free of external evaluation. Psychological freedom occurs by granting the individual permission to engage in unrestrained symbolic expression. Harrington et al. (1987) looked at child-rearing in this context. They followed 106 children and families in a longitudinal study. They categorized childrearing practices based on data collected while the children were preschoolers. The childrearing practices data were based on parent questionnaires and observations of parent–child interactions. Judges reached good agreement in categorizing the child-rearing practice items into Rogers' scheme. Some of the childrearing practice items on the parent survey that were judged as most typical of Rogers' creativity fostering environment were:

- I respect my child's opinions and encourage him or her to express them.
- My child should have time to think, daydream, and loaf
- I let my child make his or her own decisions.
- We have a warm, intimate time together.
- I encourage curiosity, exploring, and questioning.
- I make sure my child knows I appreciate what he or she tries to accomplish.

Examples of items least typical of Roger's creativity fostering environment were:

- Children should be seen and not heard.
- I do not allow my child to get angry with me.
- I do not allow questions and discussions.

Relationships were investigated between childrearing practices of the parents and a creative potential index of the child as a preschooler and as a young adolescent. The creative potential index was based on teachers' ratings and personality Q-sorts. Interestingly, there was a correlation of .33 between the preschool creative potential score and the young adolescent creative potential score, indicating some stability for this characteristic. Correlations between childrearing practices of the parents, mother alone, and father alone and creative potential for both ages were moderate in size, varying from .38 to .49. Children whose parents used childrearing practices consistent with Rogers' framework had higher creative potential scores at both ages. After using path-analytic techniques, Harrington et al. (1987) concluded that Rogers' childrearing practices techniques contributed significantly to adolescent creative potential scores after gender, IQ, and preschool creativity scores were controlled for. This finding is consistent with the view that these practices influence creative development. Harrington et al. stressed that environments that foster the child's autonomy and self-confidence should also foster creativity. They do raise the question of stages — does the child have different needs at different stages? Different environments may indeed have differential effects at different developmental stages.

The findings of this study are important because it was a well-done study in which we can put some confidence. Although the findings do not speak to affect specifically, the childrearing practice items are consistent with the principles of safety, acceptance, and permissiveness that therapists stress in helping children to express affect in play.

Harrington et al.'s (1987) findings are consistent with the work of Csikszentmihalyi (1990b). He reported on the results of a study of family context in his laboratory at the University of Chicago with Kevin Rathunde. This study investigated variables in the families of teenagers that promoted optimal experiences for creative functioning. Five major characteristics of the family context emerged:

1. Clarity of expectations — clear rules and feedback in the family interaction.
2. Centering — parents are interested in what the child is currently doing — rather than focusing too much on the future.

3. Choice — the child can choose from a variety of possibilities.
4. Commitment — trust and a secure environment enables the child to feel safe enough to set aside defenses.
5. Challenge — parents provide complex opportunities for action.

In a longitudinal study of talented children and adults, Csikszentmihalyi and Rathunde (Adler, 1991) found that a home environment that combined both support and optimal challenge was essential for creative development. Optimal challenge was also stressed by Hunt and Paraskevopoulos (1980). Csikszentmihalyi and Rathunde (Adler, 1991) found that the coexistence of these factors was important. Support helped the child feel confident and secure, so she could experiment and take risks. Challenge kept the child developing her skills. This study followed 210 high school students for 4 years. These were talented students in mathematics, science, music, sports, or art. A major finding of the study was that intrinsic motivation is central. One of their recommendations is that teachers help the child "become absorbed in the tasks."

Other factors emerge in the literature as being important for creative development. Singer and Singer (1990) reported that preschoolers who were read to or had sitting down time with their parents were more imaginative. Creative older children reported that parents told stories or played fantasy games with them. Singer and Singer followed preschoolers and did home visits for an in-depth study of parents and the home environment. Imaginative children had parents who were more resourceful, adventuresome, and creative based on self-descriptions. They used inductive childrearing, not physical discipline, and had clear rules. These parents also had more orderly routines. One might speculate that the orderly routines and clear rules established predictable limits that helped the child feel safe and calm and develop the internal structure that is so important in the preschool years. Roni Tower, a student of Singer's, studied parents of gifted children and found that parents of these children spent more time with them on school-related activities, demonstrated unconditional love, (supporting Rogers' notion) and fostered independence.

Amabile (1983) had a good review of the literature on environments that foster creativity. She cited a study by Miller and Gerard (1979) that found that families of creative individuals showed low levels of authoritarianism and encouraged independence. These parents were not so concerned with the rules and inhibitions of society. We might speculate that these children felt more confident in taking risks, following their own path, and taking unconventional stands. MacKinnon's (1962) creative architects had parents who had confidence in their children, kept interpersonal distance, and paid little attention to formal religion. Albert and Runco (1989) found that creative preadolescent boys were more independent than the control group.

Michel and Dudek (1991) found that mothers of high creative eight-year-olds were less emotionally involved with their children, less likely to be perceived as overprotective, and less likely to deny hostility toward the child. This is consistent with reports of art students that their parents allowed them to think and feel as they wished when they were children (Dudek, 1972).

The interpersonal distance factor is interesting. On the face of it, it seems contradictory to other findings of parental warmth and investment in the child as being important factors in child development. Certainly, subtle differences in the measures used in different studies could account for mixed results. However, I agree with Amabile who speculated that some appropriate distance between parents and children could increase independence and autonomy. Amabile (1983) listed the following characteristics, based on her review of the literature, as ideal qualities of a creativity-fostering home environment:

1. Children should have a choice in how to perform a task.
2. Reward should be used in such a way that it leads to positive affect and higher enjoyment of the task; reward should not be used as the sole purpose of carrying out the task.
3. Play and fantasy should be encouraged.
4. There should be sufficient distance between parents and children.

THE SCHOOL ENVIRONMENT

The school environment is one that can foster creativity, inhibit creativity, or have no effect whatsoever. A thorough review of the literature on the school environment can be found in Amabile (1983). Torrence (1967) referred to the "fourth grade slump" in creativity due to peer pressure to conform. Getzels and Jackson (1962) reported that creative children are often viewed as a bother by teachers. Boys are more likely to be viewed as creative by teachers than girls (Evans, 1979).

Amabile (1983) reviewed a study by Rosenthal, Baratz, and Hall (1974), which concluded that the following teacher characteristics were related to fostering creativity in their students: more likeable; more interested; more satisfied; more enthusiastic; more courteous; more business-like; more professional; and more encouraging. Here again, we see an interesting mix of warmth and interest and maintaining professional distance from the student.

Amabile's (1983) recommendations for teachers based on her work and the literature, were:

1. Help the child look for cues in the environment.
2. Help develop the child's talents.
3. Help the child make positive constructive evaluations of his or her work.
4. Recognize and tolerate the unusual.
5. Help the child resist peer pressure toward conformity.
6. Give a lot of choice.
7. Reduce the amount of evaluation.

Csikszentmihalyi's (1991) advice to teachers was to help the child become absorbed in the task. Singer and Singer (1985) listed a variety of make-believe games that teachers can use in the classroom. They also suggested a book by Rosenberg, (1987), which suggests games and procedures that foster imagination in school.

Educators are now stressing the importance of bringing affect back into the classroom. Snow (1991) stressed the importance of integrating the constructs of cognitive and affective aspects of learning. Currie (1988) is concerned that academic achievement is moving away from a focus on the total child and the importance of emotional development. He stressed the importance of broad affective ties in the school and the perceived warmth of the teacher based on Rohner's (1986) work.

Singer and Singer (1990) reviewed Smilansky's (1986) work with socio-dramatic play in a school setting. She worked with kindergarten children in Israel for 90 minutes a day, 5 days a week, for 9 weeks. The children who engaged in the sociodramatic play, with help from their teachers, showed significant cognitive improvement when compared with other groups. The teachers helped the children develop their play by commenting, making suggestions, and giving demonstrations. This stimulation by teachers helped the children do what they wanted to do. Actually, this is what good play therapists do with young children. They give appropriate guidance and usually, the child is drawn to developmental issues and/or conflicts that need to be worked on.

Gardner (1991) nobly called for a restructuring of the school experience. He is encouraging society to think creatively about the school environment. He feels that we must teach students in context and use approaches that help students see the reasons for learning. He suggested alternative teaching models, such as the apprenticeship model, and using places other than schools for learning, such as children's museums as supplements to the school experience. He described different teaching approaches (narrational, esthetics approach, and experiential) that are appropriate at different times for different children.

Gardner (1991) described Project Spectrum, an early childhood educa-tion program, as having different physical areas for different learning areas. There is a naturalist's area and a story-telling area. Children observe peers and adults in these different modes and areas. Recommendations are made for each child focusing on their particular needs.

Gardner's description of tracking individual students and utilizing different teaching approaches reminds me of a well-functioning open classroom setting in an elementary school in Cherry Creek School District in Denver, in the early 1970s. I was working as a consultant to this school district out of the Arapaho Mental Health Center. We worked with a number of open classroom environments, but one particular school (Walnut Hills) exemplified what a well-functioning open classroom experience should be. Although not articulated, the teachers followed many of the principles recently put forth by Gardner. From kindergarten through third grade, children were individually tracked with specific recommendations for each child. A number of different teachers were involved with these students in an open classroom setting, so a variety of teaching styles were available. There were different areas for different activities and the children frequently moved around. A mental health consulting team was also involved with the teaching team, had frequent meetings with the teaching team, spent time in the classroom environment, worked with individual children, and in essence, developed a profile of strengths and problem areas for each child with recommendations. This teaching team worked with these students for several years, so there was good continuity from year to year for each child. The goal was optimal development for each child along a variety of dimensions. Idealistic as this may sound, I have seen it work. The teaching team was impressive in that these teachers were very open to experimenting and trying different approaches. On the other hand, because there was an individual program for each child, there was much more structure than met the eye. An optimally open classroom environment includes a balance of structured and unstructured activities.

After reviewing the research on the effect of open education environments, Walberg (1988) concluded that open classrooms, "on average, enhance creativity, independence, and other nonstandard outcomes, without detracting from academic achievement unless they are radically extreme" (p. 353).

What Gardner and programs such as the Cherry Creek School Program have not specifically addressed is the question of whether guidance in the use of play and expression of affect and fantasy should be a formal part of the school curriculum for young children (kindergarten through third grade). Perhaps schools should begin to think about having "Play Centers" available for young children, kindergarten through third grade, where play facilitation techniques and fantasy games are used. The evidence suggests that these activities would spur cognitive and creative development for many children.

I think a pilot project that established a Play Center as a supplementary experience for children from kindergarten through third grade, following Gardner's model, would be a logical step at this time. Different types of play opportunities could be available so that individual needs would be accommodated. It would be crucial that the teachers and aids in the center would be expert at facilitating children's play. Because the continuity of play is so important, having regular play periods over a period of time, rather than one-shot training sessions, should be most effective. The approach used by Smilansky (1986) would be a good model for establishing such a play center. The time is right for the development of play centers. There is a wider recognition of the importance of play in cognitive and affective development. For example, in a study by Alessandri (1991), maltreated preschoolers as compared to normal children showed less play, less mature play, less symbolic play, less organized play, restricted themes, and less affect expression. There were no differences in IQ. He recommended that programs that value cognitive or social components of play within a structured setting might be useful in facilitating the overall development of maltreated preschoolers.

WORK ENVIRONMENTS AND LIFESTYLES

What can we say about fostering creativity in adulthood? From a holistic approach, Csikszentmihalyi (1990a) spoke of maximizing optimal experience, which includes his concept of "flow." An optimal flow of experience occurs when the individual is totally involved in the activity, feels a deep sense of enjoyment, and is optimally challenged in the activity. Creative activities involve this sense of flow. These activities are intrinsically rewarding or autotelic, as he puts it. The enjoyment of the act occurs when the individual experiences forward movement, a sense of novelty, accomplishment, and development of the self. He emphasized the importance of the level of challenge. He also identified flexibility and fluidity of attention as important in the flow experience.

Work environments and lifestyles that foster creativity and a sense of flow in the adult need to be developed. There has not been much empirical work in this area. Amabile (1990a) addressed this issue and reported on work with Gryskiewicz (Amabile & Gryskiewicz, 1989), which studied 120 R&D scientists in corporations. They carried out a content analysis of descriptions by the scientists of critical incidents in their work. Environmental conditions were prominent in their descriptions of factors that effected their creative functioning. Amabile and Gryskiewicz concluded that factors that inhibit creativity in scientists are: constrained choice, overemphasis of tangible rewards, expectation of evaluation, competition, perceived apathy toward the project, unclear goals, distractions, insufficient resources, time pressure, and an overemphasis on the status quo. These findings are very consistent with Amabile's experimental work on intrinsic motivation.

Factors that were perceived to enhance creative functioning were: encouragement, reinforcement and feedback, sufficient time to do the work, challenge, and freedom and control of the project. In earlier work, Amabile (1983) also found that job security, recognition, the ability to play at work, and an organizational climate conducive to new ideas and supportive of innovation and a high degree of choice were facilitative factors.

University settings should pay attention to the work of Csikszentmihalyi (1990a) and Amabile (1983, 1990a). Actually, the well-functioning university environment is set up to foster creative work in their faculty. Autonomy and choice are basic components of academic freedom. The ideal university setting would balance factors of autonomy and freedom to play and experiment with recognition and reward and investment in the scholarship and projects of the faculty. Csikszentmihalyi concluded that the major breakthroughs in science still depend on the individual, not on the research team. He stresses that university settings should remember this and create plenty of opportunities for, as he puts it, "amateur science."

It is difficult to know the right blend of pressure and free time for creative individuals. Ed Regis in his book *Who Got Einstein's Office* (1987) raised this point. He described the Institute for Advanced Study, which is an intellectual utopia for eminent scientists. There are no teaching demands in this setting. It sounds ideal in terms of the amount of focus that could be brought to one's research and scholarship, but as one of the faculty there discussed, it is hard to know if one's creative output would increase or decrease if there were daily classes and laboratory responsibilities. I would guess that it depends on the individual and the stage of his or her work at the time. Again, universities need to be flexible in responding to the needs of their individual faculty with sabbaticals, reduced teaching load at crucial times, and, perhaps, increasing demands and challenges when a productive scholar hits an especially long fallow period.

Cropley (1990) suggested that people attack everyday situations in creative ways. He thinks that this everyday activity should enhance overall creativity (and mental health) more effectively than formal training programs.

Although much has been written about societal factors that foster creativity, Simonton (1978), after an exhaustive study of creative individuals, concluded that no societal factors during the actual productive period have any significant impact. He concluded that societal factors have an impact during the developmental period. A formal education and political fragmentation were important to a certain extent. He speculated that political fragmentation provided exposure to a number of different viewpoints (Simonton, 1990b). Political instability, however, during the developmental period was a negative factor. Too much disorder probably interferes with the psychological safety factor stressed by Rogers (1954). Under severe stress, it would be difficult to experience low levels of arousal necessary for creative output (Simonton, 1990).

On the other hand, there were periods in history when there was a flourishing of creative productions in a number of different disciplines (Renaissance, Vienna at the turn of the century, Bloomsbury in the 1920s) What might be occurring during these periods that foster creativity? Robert Hughes (1991) put his finger on it in his book *The Shock of the New* when he discussed European cafes that fostered intellectual growth. He spoke of these cafes as a meeting place for exiles and outsiders – the "mandarins of change." In these cafes, there was a sharing of ideas and innovations. The mutual reinforcement of experimentation and innovation should encourage risk taking and sticking with a problem in creative individuals. It would also help bolster confidence and self-esteem in individuals struggling with frustrations and intermittent failure. In essence, the ingredients that fostered creative growth in these cafes may also operate in society-at-large during certain periods. A permissive environment that encourages and permits innovations may foster creativity in adults as well as in children. This may be especially true for women, for whom, until recently, pressure to conform to societal expectations was intense (Helson, 1990). It would be interesting to study factors at work during periods where higher numbers of women were creatively productive. Rubenstein (1991) spoke of the high cost of the creative act to the individual. For example, in science, a truly creative discovery frequently reduces the value of prior knowledge. He raised the general question of the degree of stigma for individuality in a society. One would assume gender differences in the cost to the individual of creative production in different cultures and in different domains.

What does all of this have to do with affect? A permissive environment should help foster openness to experience in adults and less repression of affect-laden thoughts. For many individuals, environmental conditions may not be important, but for many, especially women, they might be quite influential.

Although the main goal of psychotherapy is not to foster creativity, this is certainly a by-product of psychotherapy for many individuals. Many forms of psychotherapy help the individual gain access to taboo-laden primary process material and to repressed feeling states. As these memories and affect states are stirred, the associative network should be more available to the individual (using Bower's model). This process facilitates divergent thinking and flexible problem solving strategies.

Psychotherapy can also help the individual work through conflicts that are blocking creative work. Gedo (1990) had an eloquent discussion of this issue. And, there are many accounts such as Middlebrook's (1991) account of Anne Sexton, in which therapy was an integral part of the creative development of the individual.

In conclusion, as I stressed in chapter 5, there are many routes to developing creativity. Many of the affective, cognitive, and personality characteristics important in creativity are developed in the early years, through the stimulation of play and imagination, a predictable living situation, openness to affective expression, and affective investment in the child by the parents. Schools can help foster these abilities in children and can help those with deficits in these cognitive, affective, and personality dimensions make up for what they have missed, especially in the early years. In later years, the home and school environment can keep the child on track by maintaining optimal environments for creative development, and healthy development in general. As adults, we can take the initiative in following a lifestyle conducive to creative work. One can also seek psychotherapy to open up affective realms and to resolve conflicts that are getting in the way. Work settings can begin to follow some of the few guidelines that we know of and do some comparison studies. University settings, in addition to following basic principles of fostering creativity in their faculty, could establish their own version of the old European cafes. Discussion centers, in various modes, where faculty could come together informally to discuss ideas and new ventures, or to argue the issues of the day, might help develop the kind of atmosphere conducive to creative work.

9

Affective Components of the Creative Process: Conclusions and Future Research Directions

The purpose of this book was to answer two basic questions:

1. Is affect an important part of the creative process?
2. If so, how is affect involved in creative thinking?

To answer the first question, I think we can conclude that affect is important in the creative process. The empirical evidence and descriptions of creativity support theoretical assumptions that affect is important. Correlational studies have pointed to a relationship between affect and creativity. Recent empirical work is suggesting a cause and effect relationship between positive affect and creativity. Recent neurological conceptualizations of affect and cognition offer a framework for understanding why affect might facilitate creative thinking.

The second question is the more difficult one. Patterns are emerging that suggest the different ways that affect is facilitative. This question is what future research studies should address. I now review the basic patterns that have emerged in the literature and the conclusions I have put forth in this book.

Affect is important in facilitating specific cognitive processes important in creativity. Affect is also related to certain personality characteristics that have been related to creativity. Let us first review affect and cognitive processes.

AFFECT AND COGNITIVE PROCESSES

Affect probably makes its largest impact in facilitating cognitive processes that have been found to be important in creative thinking. Referring back to Fig. 1.1, the model of affect and creativity, the major cognitive abilities are:

- divergent thinking
- transformation abilities
- sensitivity to problems and problem identification
- tendency to practice with alternative solutions
- wide breadth of knowledge
- insight and synthesizing abilities
- evaluative abilities

The major affective processes are:

- access to affect-laden thoughts, including primary process
- openness to affect states
- affective pleasure in challenge
- affective pleasure in problem soling
- cognitive integration of affective material

Although it is highly likely that these affective processes are interrelated, as are the cognitive processes, these affective processes do seem to reflect different dimensions and different patterns in the empirical literature.

Access to Affect-Laden Thoughts

Access to affect-laden thoughts, affect-laden fantasy, and primary process material is related to divergent thinking and to transformation abilities. These are key processes in creative thinking and are probably, along with affect states, the major link between affect and creativity. Bower's associative network theory offers a good theoretical explanation for why access to affect-laden material should facilitate divergent thinking and transformation abilities, although he does not speak directly to the issue of creativity. Access to affect-laden thoughts, or mood-relevant cognition, would activate other memory nodes and permit a wide range of associations to occur. This would aid the search process, which is so important to divergent thinking. This broader associative ability would also benefit the transformation process, the ability to break out of an old set and see something in a new way.

In addition, the ability to tap into primary process cognition may facilitate divergent thinking and transformation abilities in a different way. The ability to get into the less controlled state of "riding the associative currents" (Wallach, 1970), of defocused attention and low cortical arousal, may be aided by comfort with primary process material and the ability to tap into a primary process-free association mode.

All of the research linking access to affect-laden thoughts to divergent thinking and transformation abilities has been correlational with children and adults. Although the consistency of the patterns of relationships is strongly suggestive of a facilitative effect, we need to carry out intervention studies that increase expression of affect-laden thoughts and use creative thinking tasks as the dependent variable. The Affect in Play Scale is one tool that could be used for this purpose. We know that altering instructions will increase different categories of affect in fantasy play. A next research step is to determine whether altering instructions alters performance on divergent thinking or transformation tasks.

Research to date has also shown gender differences with this variable. Access to affect-laden thoughts and primary process material has consistently been related to creativity measures for males, but not for females. The results for females have been mixed, more negative results than positive. In several research studies, girls expressed less primary process content than boys — both on the Rorschach and in play. One might speculate that the environment is less permissive for girls than for boys for the expression of this kind of fantasy. Thus, girls as a group may not develop the wide range of associative links that so aid the creative process, nor learn to tap into that process. Reasons behind the gender differences is another important direction for future research.

Another way access to affect-laden fantasy, particularly primitive primary process fantasy, can facilitate creativity, especially artistic creativity, is by the generation of images and affective content important in the artistic transformation process. The affect content itself is utilized to generate a universal symbol that captures universal experience.

Finally, although speculative because there is no real empirical work to back this up, access to affect-laden material could help in insight and synthesizing ability. Again, this may be especially so in artistic creativity where the synthesizing process may involve a blending of very disparate elements. Even in scientific problem solving, affect-laden cognition may be involved in the reconfiguration process.

Openness to Affect States

Openness to affect states has been found to be related to divergent thinking and transformation abilities. In addition, induced positive affect states facilitates wider associations, the ability to break sets, and analogical transfer abilities in adults. In all but one study, induced negative affect has not been found to facilitate creativity, but theory, the correlational studies, and the memory studies suggest that negative affect should also facilitate creativity. As Isen et al. (1987) suggested, less severe negative affect states than the one used in their study might have a facilitative effect. In addition, affect-laden fantasy and affect-laden thoughts may function differently from affect states. Negative affect-laden thoughts, such as aggressive images or aggressive humor, without an attached negative affect state, might be facilitative of divergent thinking and transformation abilities. However, moderate negative affect states may interfere with creative thinking. On the other hand, while in a negative mood state, one might encode a good deal of mood-relevant cognition, which one could tap into later. One is reminded of the traumatized child who then uses play to work through the material and consolidate it. The content would not be repressed, but would be available for future use.

Research with openness to affect states is only at the beginning of what needs to be done. Replications of Isen's work need to be carried out with children. Differential effects of positive and negative affect states should be explored as well as effects of subcategories of affect states (aggression, sadness, happiness, affection) on creativity.

Affective Pleasure in Challenge

Although there is not much empirical literature in this area, affective pleasure in challenge is often mentioned as being important in problem identification and in pursuing the problem. Voss and Means (1989) spoke of the anticipation of the positive affect involved in solving the problem as being the motivating force. However, there may be an inherent excitement in seeing the ambiguity in the situation that leads to problem identification, which is itself pleasurable. It may be similar to the pleasure that some children feel in discovering "what is wrong with this picture?" Runco (in press) discussed the anticipation of reducing the tension and discomfort by solving the problem as an important motivating factor in creativity.

Affective Pleasure in Problem Solving

There is a consensus in the literature that affective pleasure in problem solving is important in task persistence and in recognizing the right solution when it occurs. Amabile (1983) stressed the importance of positive affect in intrinsic motivation. This anticipated pleasure should keep the individual deeply engaged in the task. The pleasurable feeling involved in discovering the right solution or achieving the best synthesis is deeply reinforcing.

Although this construct has not been widely researched, there are so many descriptions of the positive affect involved in the creative process that it is almost a given. The profound nature of this experience is also a frequent description by creative individuals. It suggests that openness to affect states and to the capacity for passionate involvement in a task would be interrelated variables.

Cognitive Integration of Affective Material

The ability to integrate and modulate affective material reflects a largely integrative cognitive structure that enables the individual to tolerate affect states, regress in the service of the ego, and call forth critical thinking and evaluative skills throughout the creative process. This integrative ability has been found to relate to divergent thinking and transformation abilities in children and adults. Although difficult to measure (the Adaptive Regression Score on the Rorschach and the Affective Integration scores on the Affect in Play Scale are two attempts), we need to continue to tease out the cognitive and affective components of this broad-based ability. This cognitive integration ability influences the expression of and development of the other affective processes. It is probably highly related to the ability to tolerate affect, because the individual can feel in control of the affect and affect-laden thoughts. It enables the affective processes to be used adaptively, as a resource, in the creative process.

AFFECT AND PERSONALITY TRAITS

Based on the research literature, the major personality traits important in the creative process are:

- tolerance of ambiguity
- openness to experience
- possessing unconventional values
- independence of judgement
- curiosity
- preference for challenge and complexity
- self-confidence
- propensity for risk taking
- intrinsic motivation

These personality traits emerged from major research programs (Barron & Harrington, 1981) and theoretically could have some link to affective processes. Martindale (1989) stated that "creative cognition occurs only within a certain configuration of personality traits" (p. 213). I would add that the presence of these personality traits increases the likelihood that the important affective processes in creative cognition would occur. Also, some of the personality traits reflect the presence of these affective processes.

The proposed links between affect and personality traits are less empirically based than those between affect and cognition and are more speculative.

Access to affect-laden thoughts and openness to affect states are both related to openness to experience and to tolerance of ambiguity. As McCrae and Costa (1987) concluded, openness to experience is related to access to thoughts, feelings, and impulses. Access to primary process facilitates openness to experience. Tolerance of ambiguity is also related to these dimensions of affect in that a variety of disparate thoughts and feelings can be experienced simultaneously. Comfort with affect states and affective fantasy should increase the probability that the openness to experience trait would develop.

Affective pleasure in challenge would be important in the well-researched trait of preference for challenge and complexity. Pleasure in challenge would also be consistent with the trait of curiosity and risk taking. Affective pleasure in problem solving is an important component in intrinsic motivation, curiosity, and self-confidence. A self-confident individual anticipates being able to solve the problem and anticipates the positive affect involved.

We may never be able to specify the particular affective processes important in these global personality traits that are correlates of creativity. Perhaps it is not so important that we do so. Although it may useful to identify some of the affective processes associated with these global personality traits, the more important links that will shed light on creative thinking are probably the cognitive-affective links. The thrust of future research programs should be in that direction.

FUTURE RESEARCH DIRECTIONS

It is encouraging to see the recent flourishing of research in the area of creativity. Some of the recent emerging trends are: investigation of the role of affect in the creative process; the importance of children's play in fostering creativity; increased attention to the type of criterion used to measure creativity (test vs. creative product issue); more specificity to the variables being investigated; and increased recognition of the importance of an interdisciplinary approach and dialogue to achieve a more comprehensive understanding of the creative process. Real world creativity should be studied and a variety of techniques and approaches should be used to investigate creativity.

The Role of Affect in Creativity

Future research should explore the usefulness of the model of affect and creativity put forth in this book. Measures for the five affective dimensions need to be developed and refined. Are these proposed five dimensions of affect indeed different dimensions? If so, what are their developmental properties? Is there an element of heritability? Is the model comprehensive or are there other important affective processes that are missing from the model? As mentioned earlier, this model of affect and creativity is presented as an initial road map that can guide future research. Empirical links between the affective processes and cognitive processes need to be strengthened and cause and effect need to be demonstrated where it exists.

Building on the empirical foundation that has been established in this area, important future research questions are:

• Are affect-laden thoughts and affect states truly different dimensions and/or processes? If so, do they have different kinds of effects on cognitive processes?

• What are the best research paradigms for investigating these different affective processes. Mood-induction studies may be best at investigating affect states. Studies that manipulate instructions for the Rorschach, TAT, and fantasy play may be better for investigating the effect of affect-laden cognition on creative processes.

• Do different categories of affect content have differential effects on creativity?

• Are there gender differences for the effect of different kinds of affect content and affect processes on creativity? What are the reasons for the gender differences?

• Does primary process play a unique role in creative thinking, as psychoanalytic theory would suggest, or does it have the same intervention effects as standard positive and negative affect dimensions on creativity?

• Do positive and negative affect dimensions function differently for affect-laden cognition than for affect states?

• Can we begin to break down divergent thinking tasks and set breaking tasks into more specific components so we can zero-in on exactly where affective processes have their effect?

Play and Creativity

Play is being increasingly recognized as being important in fostering affective development and imagination. Singer and Singer (1990) stressed the importance of studying natural play in familiar settings. Studying natural play situations is ideal, although this is more difficult to do for the older child if we are interested in solitary fantasy play. We need to continue carrying out good longitudinal studies of children's play to learn how it aids creative functioning as well as general adjustment.

A very fruitful line of research should be investigating specific interventions in the play situation. We need to learn two things:

• What are the optimal interventions for facilitating affective expression in the experimental situation and in the therapeutic situation? Although we have many guidelines in the clinical literature about how to facilitate affect, there is little empirical work in the area.

• How do these affective interventions, in turn, effect specific creative cognitive processes?

Although we need to be careful of experimenter effects in these play studies, as Smith and Whitney warned (1987), some of the suggestions in chapter 3 address these methodological issues.

The results of these future play studies should teach us about the role of play in personality and cognitive development and provide knowledge about intervening in school and therapy settings.

Measures of Creativity

Michael and Wright (1989) have an excellent overview of measurement issues in creativity research. There seems to be a growing trend to use real life measures of creativity. Hocevar and Bachelor (1989) concluded that, although measures like divergent thinking measures are important correlates of creativity, the field needs to focus on eminence, actual creative products, or inventories of accomplishments. They caution that we should not uncritically accept divergent thinking measures, interest inventories, or creative personality measures.

Amabile (1990a; 1990b) stressed the importance of using creative products in creativity research that are rated by experts in the domain. She used what she calls the consensual assessment technique. She defined it as follows: "A product or response is creative to the extent that appropriate observers independently agree it is creative. Appropriate observers are those familiar with the domain in which the product was created or the response articulated" (Amabile, 1990b, p. 65). On the other hand, experts' judgments are not totally accurate indications of creativity. Issues arise such as who chooses the experts and who sets the criteria.

Dudek (1992) also stressed the importance of studying real world creativity and the importance of longitudinal studies of creative individuals.

Franklin (1992) discussed the value of the interview and case study method with creative individuals. Sternberg and Davidson (1985), Gardner (1983), and Feldman (1982) all stressed the value of the individual case study approach.

Given the state of the field of creativity research, we should continue to use a variety of measures and approaches to studying creativity. Tests of cognitive processes such as divergent thinking, known to be important in creativity, give us information about specific processes. Real world creative products give us different information. We need to use both, perhaps judiciously combined, so that we can learn about specific processes but also know that these processes are really involved in creativity.

Specific Versus Global Research

When I first began writing this book, I was a strong proponent of very focused studies looking at specific affective and cognitive processes. Having reviewed the literature and contemplated the issues, I now think the field needs a balance of specific studies and global studies. The field to date has progressed by blending the knowledge gathered from a variety of different approaches and should probably continue in that vein. In the affect area, we need to continue carrying out very focused studies on affect and cognition with children and adults. Perhaps these studies could then generate questions that could be focused on in interviews with creative individuals or in studying the writings of eminent individuals. For example, how did individuals who are high in openness to affect and experience learn to deal with negative experiences? How did they use play and fantasy as children? As in good clinical research, where systematic studies in the laboratory should influence clinical work and hypotheses that develop in clinical work should generate the next research study, creativity research may follow the same model.

Interdisciplinary Approach

Csikszentmihalyi (1990b) discussed the fragmentation of effort in different fields in studying creativity. He called for the integration of different disciplines and approaches. He referred to the work of Magyari-Beck (1976), which includes the role of the field and the domain in studying the creative process. Magyari-Beck's approach includes four levels in which creativity can be studied — the culture, institution, working group, and the person. Creativity can be manifested as a trait, a process, and a product. Thus, he generates a 3 × 4 matrix that could be used for studying creativity. This approach is also relevant for studying the role of affect in creativity.

Certainly, in the area of affect and creativity, an interdisciplinary approach would be useful. Even within the field of psychology, different specialty areas need to communicate better with one another and find ways to translate their concepts and language. The areas of psychoanalytic theory, social psychology, child clinical, child development, neurological psychology, and educational psychology all have different approaches to the concept of creativity and have made major contributions. We could make more progress if we pooled our knowledge and worked to integrate our constructs and approaches.

CONCLUSION

It is heartening to see the variety of avenues being taken in creativity research. There is a growing consensus in the field that affect is important in the creative process. Theoreticians and observers of the creative process have long recognized the importance of affect in creativity. Only recently has the empirical work begun to support the affect–creativity link. The field needs to continue these beginning efforts to build models of affect and creativity, to develop measures of affect, to refine research paradigms that manipulate affect, and to develop hypotheses and important research questions. As the field continues to move along in this direction, we can fill in the other half of the picture of creativity—the affect half. What a pleasure it is to be part of this evolving creative process.

Appendix: Affect in
Play Scale[1]

The Affect in Play Scale measures the amount and kinds of affective expression in children's fantasy play. The scale rates the frequency and intensity of affective expression, variety of affect categories, quality of fantasy, quality of integration of affect, and comfort in play. Play sessions are 5-minute standardized puppet play periods.

Affective expression consists of the occurrence of affective content themes and actual emotional expression. Conceptually, the Affect in Play Scale taps three dimensions of affect in fantasy:

1. Actual affective experiencing through expression of feeling states.
2. Affective content themes, including primary process themes.
3. Cognitive integration and modulation of affect. This dimension is reflected in the combination of quality of fantasy scores and affect scores.

THE PLAY TASK

It is important that the play objects and task to be observed be unstructured enough so that individual differences in fantasy play can emerge. The Play Task utilizes two neutral-looking puppets, one boy and one girl, and three

---

[1]Copyright 1985, Sandra W. Russ. Anna Grossman-McKee, Zina Rutkin, and Amir Jassani contributed to the development of the scale.

small blocks that are laid out on a table. It is administered individually to the child. The instructions for the task for the free-play period are:

> I'm here to learn about how children play. I have here two puppets and would like you to play with them any way you like for 5 minutes. For example, you can have the puppets do something together. I also have some blocks that you can use. Be sure to have the puppets talk out loud. The video camera will be on so that I can remember what you say and do. I'll tell you when to stop.

The child is informed when there is 1 minute left. If the child stops playing during the 5-minute period, the prompt, "You still have time left, keep going" is given. The task is discontinued if the child can not play after a 2-minute period.

SCORES

There are eight major scores.

1. Total frequency of units of affective expression. A unit is defined as one scorable expression by an individual puppet. In a two puppet dialogue, expressions of each puppet are scored separately.
2. Variety of affect categories. There are 11 possible affect categories, the last 6 of which are primary process categories. The categories are: Happiness/Pleasure, Anxiety/Fear, Sadness/Hurt, Frustration/Displeasure, Nurturance/Affection, Oral, Oral Aggression, Anal, Sexual, Aggression, and Competition.
3. Mean intensity of affective expression (1–5 rating).
4. Mean intensity × frequency score.
5. Comfort in play score (1-5 global rating).
6. Global quality of fantasy (1–5 rating).
7. Mean quality of fantasy, based on subscores of organization, elaboration, imagination, and repetition.
8. Affective integration scores.
   a. Mean quality & mean intensity
   b. Mean quality × frequency
   c. Mean quality & mean intensity × frequency

GENERAL PRINCIPLES FOR INTENSITY RATINGS

All of the affect intensity ratings are based on the expression of content themes and actual experiencing. "I like this hot dog" is comprised of both an affective content theme (hot dog—oral) and an emotional expression (like). In general, combinations of the emotion and content themes get higher intensity ratings than the theme alone or the emotion alone. The general criteria for the 1–5 intensity ratings are:

1. Reference to affective content alone.
2. Reference to affective content with special emphasis, which implies experiencing (such as personal referent).
3. Current experiencing, which includes:
   a. moderate action alone
   b. current feeling state with conversational voice
   c. primary process theme plus mild feeling state
4. Stronger current experiencing which includes:
   a. mild action plus mild feeling state
   b. strong action alone
   c. strong affect alone
   d. for primary process categories, unusual and strong feeling or strong theme word
   e. primary process theme and moderate affect
5. Very strong feeling state, which includes:
   a. action plus strong feeling state
   b. extreme primary process theme work, almost inappropriate
   c. extremely strong affect
   d. extremely strong action

In general, affective theme, emotional expression (word, tone, facial expression, etc.), and action are additive components.

SPECIFIC CATEGORY CRITERIA FOR INTENSITY RATINGS

Aggression

1. Reference to aggressive content.
   Ex: Here's a toy gun; here's a knife; this is broken.
2. Personalized reference to aggressive content, mild bickering.
   Ex: I have a knife; I'll break it; let's fight; no—I don't want to do that.
3. Actual fighting, hitting, tussling; destroying other's property; aggressive dialogue with feeling; angry feeling statement "I am mad."
   Ex I don't' want to do that—that's stupid (with feeling); I'll punch you; I don't like you. Let's fight (with feeling).

4. Action plus dialogue, strong feeling state; strong theme word.
   Ex: Hitting plus "You're stupid"; I hate you; here is a bomb and it's going to explode.
5. Strong action and strong dialogue; extreme emotional theme.
   Ex: I'll kill you; I'm going to beat your brains to a pulp; actions of shooting or stabbing.

Nurturance/Affection

1. Reference to nurturing affectionate themes.
   Ex: Sally and John are friends; yesterday my mom helped me.
2. Personalized nurturing theme or theme with special emphasis.
   Ex: Are you ok?; I'll help; don't forget your sweater; Sally and John are best friends.
3. Nurturing activity; current feeling state of affection.
   Ex: I like you. You're my friend; gift-giving; patting; helping, handshake.
4. Action plus dialogue; strong verbal statement or strong action.
   Ex: Hugging; dancing; I really like you; you're my very best friend.
5. Strong action plus strong dialogue; very strong nurturing action or word.
   Ex: I love you; I really like you (while patting or hugging).

Happiness/Pleasure

1. Reference to content involving happiness, pleasure, satisfaction, general preference statements.
   Ex: That dress is pretty; Saturday is the best day of the week; that's nice.
2. Reference with special emphasis; personalized; affective content distanced by past/future or 3rd person tense. Subjective references to fun and amusement.
   Ex: Johnny looks happy; that was fun; oh boy, the circus is in town; that's good; I like this red hair.
3. Current affective experiencing or activity involving happiness, pleasure. Happiness themes plus feeling state.
   Ex: I feel happy (conversational); hand-clapping; I love to get presents; I like this (with strong tone); this is fun.
4. Activity plus affective expression. Strong feeling state; strong action alone (jumping up and down with happy expression).
   Ex: I feel happy (more than conversational); it's so wonderful to be happy; whee, this is fun; I really like that; I love this.

5. Combination of two of the following: emotional expression, theme, or activity (at least one at extreme level or 2 at strong level). Extreme emotional wording also scored.
   Ex: I love this (with action); Jumping and laughing.

Anxiety/Fear

1. Referent to fearful theme.
   Ex: Oh — it's time for school; it's time to go to the doctor.
2. Mild anticipation with hint of negative consequence.
   Ex: Oh no — I broke the teacher's ruler; uh-oh, I dropped my book.
3. Fearful theme with mild affect; more direct references to consequences; withdrawal or fleeing activity.
   Ex: We're gonna get in trouble; let's hide; there's a monster over there; I see a ghost.
4. Clear expression of fear; combination of theme and strong affect.
   Ex: I'm scared; the monster's coming after me; Mom's gonna spank me (with feeling).
5. Withdrawal activity plus fear; strong theme plus fearful affect.
   Ex: I'm scared, he'll kill us; don't let him hurt me (while hiding).

Sadness/Hurt

1. Nonpersonalized reference to sadness/hurt (conversational tone).
   Ex: Sally got hurt yesterday; Joe was in the hospital.
2. Personalized reference to sadness/hurt (conversational) or nonpersonalized reference with exclamation.
   Ex: Sally was crying yesterday?; sometimes I cry.
3. Current experience of sadness/hurt stated in conversational tone; action of sadness/hurt.
   Ex: That's sad; that hurts; I'm sad; I have a headache; please don't leave me.
4. Statement of sadness/hurt with sad/hurt action; stronger verbal statement; more intense sad action (experiencing).
   Ex: Ouch that hurts!; boy am I sad; please don't leave me!; whimpering, whining.
5. Strong verbal statement of sadness/hurt with action; use of very strong sad/hurt words; or very intense current experiencing of sadness/hurt.
   Ex: crying-sobbing-moaning in pain; that hurts (while crying); I don't what to go (while crying).

Frustration/Disappointment/Dislike

1. Reference to frustration/disappointment; nonpersonalized statement of frustration/disappointment (conversation voice).
   Ex: It fell; math is boring; she seems bored.
2. Personalized statement of frustration/disappointment (conversational). Nonpersonalized statement (with exclamation).
   Ex: I'm not good at building; I'm not a good drawer; it fell (with affect).
3. Current experience of frustration/disappointment (conversational tone); current action of frustration/disappointment.
   Ex: This is hard; I'm bored; I can't do this; clicking tongue.
4. Statement of frustration/disappointment with an action: statement of current experience of frustration/disappointment (exclamation); stronger action of frustration/disappointment.
   Ex: I can't get this (while knocking down blocks); boy is this hard!; this is a rotten day; oh darn!
5. Stronger statement of frustration/disappointment with an action: very strong statement of experiencing frustration/ disappointment; very strong action of frustration/disappointment.
   Ex: Slamming down the blocks while saying, "I can't do this!" — crying in frustration; swearing; I hate this!

Competition

1. Reference to competitive games.
   Ex: Mentioning cops and robbers, checkers, hide and seek.
2. Personal reference to competitive games.
   Ex: Let's play tag; let's see who can run the fastest.
3. Game playing with action, competitive theme with mild affect.
   Ex: Playing hide and seek; I like to win; I don't want to lose; I like to play tag.
4. Action plus affect; strong feeling state.
   Ex: Playing tag and saying "I win"; I'm going to beat you (with feeling); playing tag and saying, "Got you".
5. Action plus strong feeling state.
   Ex: Playing tag and then saying, "I'm king of the mountain."

Oral

1. Reference to oral content — food, cooking, mouth, stomach.
   Ex: Here's an ice cream shop; this is a new special cheese; here's your mouth.

2. Personalized reference to oral content or content with special emphasis.

   Ex: Let's eat dinner; I'll feed you; there's an ice cream shop!; Johnny is hungry.

3. Current experiencing that includes eating behavior or emotional word in conjunction with oral content.

   Ex: I like candy; I am hungry; I don't like spaghetti; that food looks good; actual eating behavior.

4. Eating behavior plus affective content; oral theme word plus moderate affective expression in voice or facial expression.

   Ex: Mmmmmmm — this is good candy; I hate spaghetti; this soup is yechy; I really like cake.

5. Strong eating behavior plus strong affective expression.

   Ex: Wow this is great (while eating); this soup is awful (while eating).

Oral Aggression

1. Reference to oral-aggressive themes.

   Ex: Teeth, dentist, poison, Dracula.

2. Personal referent to oral aggressive theme; more intense theme word; special emphasis.

   Ex: Let's go to the dentist; my tooth hurts; that dog has big teeth; he'll bite me.

3. Reference plus mild affect; activity.

   Ex: Sticking out tongue, biting; I'll bite you (with feeling).

4. Reference plus strong affect; activity plus affect.

   Ex: Biting with feeling; this is poison (yech).

5. Very strong affect and activity.

   Ex: Eating people; Dracula attacks other puppet and bites.

Anal

1. Reference to anal content (i.e., cleanliness, making a mess, dirt, sloppy).

   Ex: This is a mess; that's dirty; it's time to clean up.

2. Personalized reference to anal content or impersonal reference with special emphasis.

   Ex: I made a mess; I'll get dirty; be careful not to make a mess (special emphasis with be careful).

3. Reference to anal content plus mild affect.

   Ex: That's a real mess!; I don't like dirt; I like to play in the mud.

4. Anal activity plus feeling state; anal theme plus strong feeling state.
   Ex: I really like making a mess; yech—this is a mess; gross—how can you play in the mud; anal jokes.
5. Strong anal activity plus strong current experiencing; extreme anal theme word; strong expression of disgust around dirt; sense of inappropriate reference.
   Ex: Oh-how-awful, look at this mess; look, he pooped.

Sexual

1. Reference to mild sexual material.
   Ex: Look at his lips.
2. Personalized referent of referent with special emphasis.
   Ex: I'm going to get undressed; puppets sleeping together with sexual overtones; Sally and Joe are boyfriend and girlfriend; reference to dates.
3. Mild activity or sexual content with feeling state.
   Ex: I like to kiss; hugging if sexual context.
4. Sexual activity plus feeling, or strong sexual content.
   Ex: Dancing; kissing; looking under dress.
5. Extreme sexual content or strong activity.
   Ex: Strong kissing; blatant sexual jokes; reference to genitalia.

QUALITY OF FANTASY

Organization (Rate from 1 to 5):

1. Series of unrelated events.
2. Some cause and effect; series of loosely related events.
3. Cause and effect, organized in a temporal sequence, but no overall integrated plot.
4. More cause and effect, close to an integrated plot.
5. Integrated plot with beginning, middle, and end.

Elaboration (Rate from 1 to 5):

1. Boring, simple themes with no embellishment.
2. Minimal embellishment.
3. Much embellishment, but only in one or two dimensions.
4. Moderate embellishment across many dimensions.
5. Much embellishment across many dimensions—many details, high activity, sound effects, changes in voice, lots of facial expression and verbal inflection.

Imaginativeness (Rate from 1 to 5):

1. Based primarily on daily experience; no "new twists."
2. Several events slightly removed from daily experience (e.g., eating in a restaurant).
3. Many events slightly removed from daily experience or reference to a common childhood fantasy as being a fantasy (e.g., "Let's pretend to be cops and robbers").
4. Use of common childhood fantasy.
5. New twist on common childhood fantasy or uncommon childhood fantasy.

Repetitiveness (Rate from 1 to 5):

1. Very repetitive; perseverative quality (e.g., "This is a dog," "This is a house," etc., over and over).
2. Very repetitive, but less perseverative quality.
3. Moderate amount of repetition- similar themes, but differences within them (e.g., going to school several times, but doing something different each time—field trip, math, recess).
4. Moderate amount of repetition—less similar themes.
5. Not repetitive.

Overall Quality (Rate from 1 to 5):

This is a global rating that is made after reviewing the play rating period. It is based upon a weighted combination of the above four quality dimensions. The organization dimension is used as an anchor point. All of the other dimensions are used to either inflate or deflate the score.

Overall Comfort (Rate from 1 to 5):

This is a global rating that is made after reviewing the play rating period. The lower end of the scale considers comfort more than enjoyment, whereas the higher ratings weigh pleasure and involvement more heavily.

1. Reticent; distressed.
2. Some reticence; stiffness.
3. O.K., but not enjoying or involved.
4. Comfortable and involved.
5. Very comfortable, involved, and enjoying.

References

Adaman, J. (1991). *The effects of induced mood on creativity*. Unpublished masters thesis, University of Miami, Coral Gables, Florida.

Adler, T. (1991, September). Support and challenge: Both key for smart kids. *APA Monitor*, pp. 10-11.

Albert, R. S. (1980). Family positions and the attainment of eminence. *Gifted Child Quarterly, 24*, 87-95.

Albert, R. S., & Runco, M. A. (1989). Independence and the creative potential of giftedness and exceptionally gifted boys. *Journal of Youth and Adolescence, 18,* 221-230.

Alessandri, S. (1991). Play and social behavior in maltreated preschoolers. *Development and Psychopathology, 3,* 191-205.

Alvin, R. (1980, November). David Elkind: Going beyond Piaget. *APA Monitor,* pp. 4-5.

Amabile, T. (1983). *The social psychology of creativity*. New York: Spinger-Veclay

Amabile, T. (1990a, August). *Mechanisms of creativity: Motivation, affect, and cognition.* Paper presented at the meeting of the American Psychological Association, Boston.

Amabile, T. (1990b). Within you, without you: The social psychology of creativity and beyond. In M. Runco & R. Albert (Eds.), *Theories of Creativity* (pp. 61-91). Newbury Park, CA: Sage.

Amabile, T., & Gryskiewicz, N. (1989). The creative environment scales: Work environment inventory. *Creativity Research Journal, 2,* 231-253.

Ames, L., & Walker, R. (1964) Prediction of later reading ability from kindergarten Rorschach and IQ scores. *Journal of Educational Psychology, 55,* 309-313.

Anastasi, A., & Schaefer, C. (1969). Biological correlates of artistic and literary creativity in adolescent girls. *Journal of Applied Psychology, 53,* 267-273.

Andreasen, N. J. C. & Canter, A. (1974). The creative writer: Psychiatric symptoms and family history. *Comprehension Psychiatry, 15,* 123-131.

Arieti, S. (1976). *Creativity: The magic synthesis.* New York: Basic Books.

Arlin, P. K. (1986). Problem finding and young adult cognition. In R. A. Mines & K. S. Kitchener (Eds.), *Adult cognitive development* (pp. 22-32). New York: Praeger.

Arlow, J., & Brenner, C. (1964). *Psychoanalytic concepts and structural theory.* New York: International Universities Press.

Armbruster, B. (1989). Metacognition in creativity. In S. Glover, R. Ronning, & C. Reynolds, (Eds.), *Handbook of creativity*. (pp 177–182). New York: Plenum.

Axline, V. (1947). *Play therapy* Boston: Houghton Mifflin.

Bandura, A. (1965). Influence of models' reinforcement contingencies in the acquisition of imitative responses. *Journal of Personality and Social Psychology, 1,* 589–595.

Banks, J. T. (Ed.). (1989). *Congenial spirits: The selected letters of Virginia Woolf.* New York: Harcourt Brace Jovanovich. (Reprinted in *New York Times,* September 1991, Section 7, p. 27; Original work published 1920)

Barron, F. (1969). *Creative person and the creative process.* New York: Holt, Rinehart & Winston.

Barron, F. (1988). Putting creativity to work. In R. Sternberg (Ed.), *The nature of creativity* (pp. 76–98). Cambridge: Cambridge University Press.

Barron, F., & Harrington, D. (1981). Creativity, intelligence, and personality. In M. Rosenzweig & L. Porter (Eds.), *Annual Review of Psychology,* (Vol. 32, pp. 439–476). Palo Alto, CA: Annual Reviews.

Beard, D. (1983, May 22). Jorge Luis Borges: What else can I do but write? *The Plain Dealer,* pp. 1–7.

Begley, S. (1991, November). Thinking looks like this. *Newsweek.*

Berlyne, D. E. (1966). Conflict and arousal. *Scientific American, 215,* 82–87.

Blatt, S., Allison, O., & Feirstein, A. (1969). The capacity to cope with cognitive complexity. *Journal of Personality, 37,* 269–288.

Bower, G. H. (1981). Mood and memory. *American Psychologist, 36,* 129–148.

Bush, M. (1969). Psychoanalysis and scientific creativity. *Journal of American Psychoanalytic Association, 17,* 136–191.

Cattell, R. B. (1966). The personality and motivation of the researcher from measurements of contemporaries and from biography. In. C. W. Taylor & F. Barron (Eds.), *Scientific creativity: Its recognition and development.* (pp. 119–131). New York: Wiley.

Cattell, R. B. & Butcher, H. J. (1968). *The prediction of achievement and creativity.* Indianapolis: Bobbs-Merrill.

Cattell, R. B., & Jaspers, J. (1967). A general plasmode for factor analytic exercises and research. *Multivariate Behavioral Research Monograph, 67*(3, No. 30-10-5-2).

Claridge, G., Canter, S., & Hume, W. I. (1973). *Personality differences and biological variation: A study of twins.* Oxford: Pergamon Press.

Clark, D., & Teasdale, J. (1982). Diurnel variation in clinical depression and accessibility of memories of positive and negative experiences. *Journal of Abnormal Psychology, 91,* 87–95.

Clement, J. (1989). Learning via model construction and criticism. In J. Glover, R. Ronning, & C. R. Reynolds (Eds.), *Handbook of Creativity* (pp. 341–381). New York: Plenum.

Cohen, I. (1961). Adaptive regression, dogmatism, and creativity. *Dissertation Abstracts, 21,* 3522–3523.

Corliss, R. (1987, December). Playtime for Gonzo. *Time,* p. 75.

Cropley, A. (1990). Creativity and mental health in everyday life. *Creativity Research Journal, 3,* 167–178.

Crutchfield, R. (1962). Conformity and creative thinking. In H. Gruber, G. Terrell, & M. Wertheimer (Eds.), *Contemporary approaches to creative thinking* (pp. 120–140). New York: Atherton Press.

Csikszentmihalyi, M. (1975). *Beyond boredom and anxiety.* San Fransico: Jossey-Bass.

Csikszentmihalyi, M. (1988) Motivation and creativity: Toward a syntheses of structural and energistic approaches to cognition. *New Ideas in Psychology, 6,* 159–176.

Csikszentmihalyi, M. (1990a). *Flow: The psychology of optimal experience.* Grand Rapids, MI: Harper & Row.

Csikszentmihalyi, M. (1990b). The domain of creativity. In M. A. Runco & R. S. Albert (Eds.), *Theories of creativity.* (pp. 190–212). Newbury Park, CA: Sage.

Csikszentmihalyi, M., & Getzels, J. W. (1973). The personality of young artists: A theoretical and empirical exploration. *British Journal of Psychology, 64,* 91–104.

Culbane, J. (1988, January 10). Throw away the script. *The Plain Dealer,* pp. 1–5.

Currie, J. (1988). Affect in the schools: A return to the most basic of basics. *Childhood Education,* pp. 83–87.

Dansky, J. (1980). Make-believe: A mediator of the relationship between play and associative fluency. *Child Development, 51,* 576–579.

Dansky, J., & Silverman, F. (1973). Effects of play on associative fluency in preschool-aged children. *Developmental Psychology, 9,* 38–43.

Dorfman, E. (1951). Play therapy. In C. Rogers (Ed.), *Client-centered therapy* (pp. 235–277). Boston: Houghton Press.

Drevdahl, J. E., & Cattell, R. B. (1958). Personality and creativity in artists and writers. *Journal of Clinical Psychology, 14,* 107–111.

Dudek, S. (1968). Regression and creativity. *Journal of Nervous and Mental Disease, 147,* 535–546.

Dudek, S. (1972). *The artist's early parental relationships.* Paper presented at the meeting of the Society for Psycho-Education, Concordea, Montreal.

Dudek, S. (1975). Regression in the service of the ego in young children. *Journal of Personality Assessment, 39,* 369–376.

Dudek, S. (1980). Primary process ideation. In R. H. Woody (Ed.), *Encyclopedia of Clinical Assessment* (Vol. 1, pp. 520–539). San Francisco: Jossey-Bass.

Dudek, S. (1984). The architect as person: A Rorschach image. *Journal of Personality Assessment, 48,* 597–605.

Dudek, S. (1991). *Passion and committment in creative artists and architects.* Paper presented at the meeting of the Society For Personality Assessment, New Orleans.

Dudek, S. (1992). *Drive-derivatives and evidence of defensive flexibility in artists and architects.* Paper presented at meeting of Society for Personality Assessment, Washington, DC.

Dudek, S., & Verreault, R. (1989). The creative thinking and ego functioning of children. *Creativity Research Journal, 2,* 64–86.

Duncker, K. (1945). On problem solving. *Psychological Monographs, 58* (5, Whole No. 270).

Easterbrook, J. A. (1959). The effect of emotion on cue utilization and the organization of behavior. *Psychological Review, 66,* 183–201.

Erikson, E. N. (1963). *Childhood and society.* New York: Norton.

Evans, T. D. (1979). Creativity, sex-role socialization, and pupil–teacher interactions in early schooling. *Sociological Review, 27,* 139–155.

Exner, J. (1974). *The Rorschach: A comprehensive system.* New York: Wiley.

Fein, G. C. (1981). Pretend play in childhood: An integrative review. *Child Development, 52,* 1095–1118.

Feist, G. (1991). Synthetic and analytic thought: Similarities and differences among art and science students. *Creativity Research Journal, 2,* 145–155.

Feldman, D. H. (1982). *Developmental approaches in giftedness and creativity.* San Francisco: Josey-Bass.

Festinger, L. (1962). Cognitive dissonance. *Scientific American, 207,* 93–102.

Fischer, K. & Pipp, S. (1984). The unconscious and psychopathology. In K. S. Bowers & D. Meichenbaum (Eds.), *The unconscious reconsidered* (pp. 88–148). New York: Wiley.

Franklin, M. (1992, August). *Making Sense: Interviews and the narrative representation of artists' work.* Paper presented at meetings of the American Psychological Association, Washington, DC.

Freedheim, D., & Russ., S. (1983). Psychotherapy with children. In C. Walker & M. Roberts (Eds.), *Handbook of clinical child psychology* (pp. 978–994). New York: Wiley.

Freedheim, D., & Russ., S. (1992). Psychotherapy with children. In C. Walker & M. Roberts (Eds.), *Handbook of clinical child psychology* (2nd ed., pp. 765–781). New York: Wiley.

Freud, A. (1965). *Normality and pathology in childhood: Assessment of development.* New York: International Universities Press.

Freud, S. (1958). The unconscious. In J. Strachey (Ed. and Trans.), *The standard edition of the complete psychological works of Sigmund Freud* (Vol. 14, pp. 159-215). London: Hogarth Press. (Original work published 1915)

Freud, S. (1959). Inhibition, symptoms, and anxiety. In J. Strachey (Ed. and Trans.), *The standard edition of the complete psychological works of Sigmund Freud* (Vol. 20, pp. 87-172). London: Hogarth Press. (Original work published 1926)

Freud, S. (1966). Project for a scientific psychology. In J. Strachey (Ed. and Trans.), *The standard edition of the complete psychological works of Sigmund Freud* (Vol. 1, pp. 283-413). London: Hogarth Press. (Original work published 1895)

Gamble, K., & Kellner, H. (1968). Creative functioning and cognitive regression. *Journal of Personality and Social Psychology, 9,* 266-271.

Gardner, H. (1983). *Frames of mind: The theory of multiple intelligences.* New York: Basic Books.

Gardner, H. (1991). *The unschooled mind.* New York: Basic Books.

Gardner, R., & Moriarity, A. (1968). *Personality development at preadolescence.* Seattle: University of Washington Press.

Gedo, J. (1990). More on creativity and its vicissitudes. In M. Runco & R. Albert (Eds.), *Theories of Creativity* (pp. 35-45). Newbury Park, CA: Sage.

Getzels, S., & Csikszentmihalyi, M. (1976). *The Creative Vision: A longitudinal study of problem finding in art.* New York: Wiley-Interscience.

Getzels, J., & Jackson, P. (1962). *Creativity and intelligence: Explorations with gifted students.* New York: Wiley.

Ghiselin, B. (1952). *The creative process.* Berkeley: University of California Press.

Ginott, H. (1965) *Between parent and child.* New York: Macmillan.

Giovacchini, P. (1960). On scientific creativity. *Journal of the American Psychoanalytic Association, 8,* 407-426.

Golann, S. E. (1963). *Psychological study of creativity. Psychological Bulletin, 60,* 548-565.

Gough, H. (1979). A creative personality scale for the Adjective Checklist. *Journal of Personality & Social Psychology, 37,* 1398-1405.

Gough, H. (1988, March). *Gender related descriptions by self and others.* Paper presented at the meeting of Society for Personality Assessment, New Orleans.

Greene, T., & Noice, H. (1988). Influence of positive affect upon creative thinking and problem solving in children. *Psychological Reports, 63,* 895-898.

Grossman-McKee, A. (1985). *Affective expression in fantasy play and its relationship to divergent thinking and achievement: An exploration of sex differences among first and second grade children.* Unpublished masters thesis, Case Western Reserve University, Cleveland, OH.

Grossman-McKee, A. (1989). The relationship between affective expression in fantasy play and pain complaints in first and second grade children. *Dissertation Abstracts international, 50.*

Gruber, H. E. (1989). The evolving systems approach to creativity work. In D. B. Wallace & H. Gruber (Eds.), *Creative people at work* (pp. 3-24). Oxford University press.

Gruber, H. E., & Davis, S. (1988). Inching our way up Mount Olympus: The evolving systems approach to creative thinking. In R. Sternberg (Ed.), *The nature of creativity.* (pp. 243-270). Cambridge: Cambridge University Press.

Guilford, J. P. (1950). Creativity. *American Psychologist, 5,* 444-454.

Guilford, J. P. (1959). *Personality.* New York: McGraw-Hill.

Guilford, J. P. (1967). *The nature of human intelligence.* New York: McGraw Hill.

Guilford, J. P. (1968). *Intelligence, creativity and their educational implications.* San Diego: Knapp.

Harrington, D. M., Block, J. W., & Block, J. (1987). Testing aspects of Carl Roger's theory of creative environments: Childrearing antecedences of creative environments in young adolescents. *Journal of Personality and Social Psychology, 52,* 851–856.

Harter, S. (1985). *Manual for the Self-Perception Profile for Children.* Denver, CO: University of Denver.

Hayes, J. (1978). *Cognitive psychology: Thinking and creating.* Homewood, IL: Dorsey Press.

Heinicke, C. (1969). Frequency of psychotherapeutic session as a factor affecting outcome: Analysis of clinical rating and test results. *Journal of Abnormal Psychology, 74,* 553–560.

Heinzen, T. (1989). On moderate challenge increasing ideational creativity. *Creativity Research Journal, 2,* 223–226.

Helson, R. (1968). Effects of sibling characteristics and parental values on creative interest and achievement. *Journal of Personality, 36,* 589–607.

Helson, R. (1971). Women mathematicians and the creative personality. *Journal of Consulting and Clinical Psychology, 36,* 210–220.

Helson, R. (1985). Which of those young women with creative potential became productive? Personality in college and characteristics of parents. In R. Hogan & W. H. Jones (Eds.), *Perspectives in personality: Theory, measurement, and interpersonal dynamics* (Vol. 1, pp. 49–80). Greenwich, CT: JAI Press.

Helson, R. (1990). Creativity in women: Outer and inner views over time. In M. Runco & R. Albert (Eds.), *Theories of creativity* (pp. 46–58). Newbury Park, CA: Sage.

Hocevar, D., & Bachelor, P. (1989). A taxonomy and critique of measurements used in the study of creativity. In. J. Glover, R. Ronning, & C. Reynolds (Eds.), *Handbook of creativity* (pp. 53–76). New York: Plenum.

Holt, R. (1967). The development of the primary process: A structural view. In R. Holt (Ed.), *Motivation and thought* (pp. 344–384). New York: International Universities Press.

Holt, R. R. (1977). A method for assessing primary process manifestations and their control in Rorschach responses. In M. Rickers-Ovsiankina (Ed.), *Rorschach psychology* (pp. 375–420). New York: Kreiger Publisher.

Holt, R. R., & Havel, J. (1960). A method for assessing primary and secondary process in the Rorschach. In M. Rickers-Ovsiankina (Ed.), *Rorschach psychology* (pp. 283–315). New York: Wiley.

Howe, P., & Silvern, L. (1981). Behavioral observation of children during play therapy: Preliminary development of research instrument. *Journal of Personality Assessment, 45,* 168–182.

Hudspith, S. (1985). *The neurological correlates of creative thought: A comparison of the EEG activity of high and low creative subjects with an ergonomic presentation of the results for the lay person.* Unpublished doctoral dissertation, University of Southern California, Los Angeles.

Hughes, R. (1991) *The shock of the new.* New York: Knopf.

Hunt, J., & Paraskevopoulos, J. (1980). Children's psychological development as a function of the inaccuracy of their mother's knowledge of their abilities. *Journal of Genetic Psychology, 136,* 285–298.

Isen, A. (1985). The asymmetry of happiness and sadness in effects on memory in normal college students. *Journal of Experimental Psychology: General, 114,* 388–391.

Isen, A., & Daubman, K. (1984). The influence of affect in categorization. *Journal of Personality and Social Psychology, 47,* 1206–1217.

Isen, A., & Daubman, K., & Nowicki G. (1987). Positive affect facilitates creative problem solving. *Journal of Personality and Social Psychology, 52,* 1122–1131.

Isen, A. M., Shalker, T. E., Clark, M., & Karp, L. (1978). Affect, accessibility of material in memory, and behavior: A cognitive loop? *Journal of Personality and Social Psychology, 36,* 1–12.

Izard, C. E. (1977). *Human emotions.* New York: Plenum.

James, W. (1890). *The principle of psychology.* New York: Holt.

Jamison, K. (1989). Mood disorders and patterns of creativity in British writers and artists. *Psychiatry, 52,* 125-134.

Jausovec, N. (1989) Affect in analogical transfer. *Creativity Research Journal, 2,* 255-266.

Johnson, G. (1990). New mind, no clothes (Review of *The Emperor's new mind*). *The Sciences, 30,* 45-49.

Julisch, B. & Krause, W. (1976) Semanlischer Kontext and Problem losungsproz esse [Semantic context and processes of resolving problems]. In F. Klix (Ed.), *Psychologische Beitrage zu Analyse Kognitiner prozesse* (pp. 116-145). Berlin: VEB Dentscher Berlay der Wissenschaften.

Kagan, J., & Moss, H. A. (1962). *Birth to maturity: A study in psychological development.* New York: Wiley.

Klein, G. (1970). *Perception, motives, and personality.* New York: Knopf.

Kleinman, M., & Russ, S. (1988). Primary process thinking and anxiety in children. *Journal of Personality Assessment, 52,* 539-548.

Klinger, E. (1971). *Structure and functions of fantasy.* New York: Wiley-Interscience.

Kogan, N. (1974). Creativity and sex differences. *The Journal of Creative Behavior, 8,* 1-14.

Kogan, N. (1976). *Cognitive styles in infancy and early childhood.* Hillsdale, NJ: Lawrence Erlbaum Associates.

Kogan, N. (1983). Stylistic variation in childhood and adolescence: Creativity, metaphor, and cognitive styles. In P. Mussen (Ed.), *Handbook of child psychology,* (Vol. 3, pp. 631-706). New York: Wiley.

Kogan, N., & Morgan, F. T. (1969). Task and motivational influences on the assessment of creative and intellective ability in children. *Genetic Psychology Monographs, 80,* 91-127.

Kris, E. (1952). *Psychoanalytic exploration in art.* New York: International Universities Press.

Krystal, H., & Krystal, A. (in press). In M. Shaw & M. Runco (Eds.), *Creativity and Affect.* Norwood, NJ: Ablex.

Kuhn, T. (1962). *The structure of scientific revolutions.* Chicago: University of Chicago Press.

Lange-Eichbaum, W. (1932). *The problem of genius* (E. Paul & C. Paul, Trans.). New York: Macmillan.

Langley, P., & Jones, R. (1988). A computational model of scientific insight. In R. Sternberg (Ed.), *The nature of creativity* (pp. 177-201). Cambridge: Cambridge University Press.

Lazarus, R. (1991). *Emotion and adaptation.* Oxford: Oxford University Press.

Leavitt, E. (1956). The water-jar Einstellung test as a measure of rigidity. *Psychological Bulletin, 53,* 547-570.

LeDoux, J. E. (1989). Cognitive-emotional interactions in the brain. *Cognition and Emotion, 3*(4), 267-289.

Lieberman, J. N. (1977). *Playfulness: Its relationship to imagination and creativity.* New York: Academic Press.

Luchins, A., & Luchins, E. (1959). *Rigidity of behavior.* Oregon: University of Oregon Books.

Maccoby, E., & Jacklin, C. (1974). *The psychology of sex differences.* Stanford, CA: Stanford University Press.

MacKinnon, D. W. (1962). The nature and nurture of creative talent. *American Psychologist, 17,* 484-495.

MacKinnon, D. W. (1965). Personality and the realization of creative potential. *American Psychologist, 20,* 273-281.

Maddi, S. (1965). Motivational aspects of creativity. *Journal of Personality, 33,* 330-347.

Magyari-Beck, I. (1976). *Kiserlit a tudomanyos alkotoas Produkt umanak Interdiszciplinaris Maghatarozasara.* Budapest: Akademia Kiado.

Martindale, C. (1981). *Cognition and consciousness.* Homewood, IL: The Dorsey Press.

Martindale, C. (1989). Personality, situation, and creativity. In J. Glover, R. Ronning, & C. R. Reynolds (Eds), *Handbook of creativity* (pp. 211-232). New York: Plenum.

Martindale, C. (1990). Creative imagination and neural activity. In R. Kunzendorf & A.

Scheifkh (Eds.), *Psychophysiology of mental imagery: Theory research and application* (pp. 89–108). Amityville, NY: Baywood.

Martindale, C., & Hasenfus, N. (1978). EEG differences as a function of creativity, stage of the creative process, and effort to be original. *Biological Psychology, 6,* 157–167.

Martindale, C., & Hines, D. (1975). Creativity and cortical activation during creative, intellectual, and EEG feedback tasks. *Biological Psychology, 3,* 71–80.

Masters, J., Barden, R., & Ford, M. (1979). Affective states, expressive behavior, and learning in children. *Journal of Personality and Social Psychology, 37,* 380–390.

Masters, J., Felleman, E., & Barden, R. (1981). Experimental studies of affective states in children. In B. Lahey & A. Kazdin (Eds.), *Advances in clinical child psychology* (pp. 91–118). New York: Plenum.

McCrae, R. R. (1987). Creativity, divergent thinking, and openness to experience. *Journal of Personality and Social Psychology, 52,* 1258–1265.

McCrae, R. R., & Costa, P.T. , Jr., (1987). Validation of the five-factor model across instruments and observers. *Journal of Personality and Social Psychology, 52,* 81–90.

McCrae, R. R., & Costa, P. T., Jr. (in press). Conceptions and correlates of openness to experience. In S. R. Briggs, W. H. Jones, & R. Hogan (Eds.), *Handbook of personality psychology.* New York: Academic Press.

McNeil, T. F. (1971). Prebirth and postbirth influences on the relationship between creative ability and recorded mental illness. *Journal of Personality, 39,* 391–406.

Mednick, S. (1962). The associative bases of the creative process. *Psychology Review, 69,* 220–232.

Mendelsohn, G. A. (1976). Associative and attentional processes in creative performance. *Journal of Personality, 44,* 341–369.

Metcalfe, J. (1986). Feeling of knowing in memory and problem solving. *Journal of Experimental Psychology: Learning, Memory, and Cognition, 12,* 288–294.

Michael, W. & Wright, C. (1989). Psychometric issues in the assessment of creativity. In J. Glover, R. Ronning, & C. Reynolds (Eds.), *Handbook of Creativity* (pp. 33–52). New York: Plenum.

Michel, M., & Dudek, S. (1991) Mother-Child relationships and creativity. *Creativity Research Journal, 4,* 281–286.

Middlebrook, D. W. (1991). *Anne Sexton.* Boston: Houghton Mifflin.

Milgram, R. (1990). Creativity: An idea whose time has come and gone? In M. A. Runco & R. S. Albert (Eds.), *Theories of Creativity* (pp. 215–233). Newbury Park, CA: Sage.

Miller, B. C., & Gerard, D. (1979). Family influences on the development of creativity in children: An integrative review. *Family coordinator, 28,* 295–312.

Milos, M., & Reiss, S. (1982). Effects of three play conditions on separation anxiety in young children. *Journal of Consulting and Clinical Psychology, 50,* 389–395.

Mischel, W. , Ebbesen, E., & Zeiss, A. (1972). Cognitive and attentional mechanisms in delay of gratification. *Journal of Personality and Social Psychology, 21,* 204–218.

Mitchell, A. R. (1972). *Schizophrenia: The meaning of madness.* New York: Taplinger.

Moore B., & Isen, A. (1990). Affect and social behavior. In B. Moore & A. Isen. *Affect and Social Behavior* (pp. 1–21). Cambridge: Cambridge University Press.

Moustakas, C. (1953). *Children in play therapy.* New York: McGraw-Hill.

Murray, J., & Russ, S. (1981). Adaptive regression and types of cognitive flexibility. *Journal of Personality Assessment, 45,* 59–65.

Natale, M., & Hanlas, M. (1982). Effect of temporary mood states on selective memory about the self. *Journal of Personality and Social Psychology, 42,* 922–934.

Niederland, W. (1973). Psychoanalytic concepts of creativity and aging. *Journal of Geriatric Psychiatry, 6,* 160–168.

Niederland, W. (1976). Psychoanalytic approaches to artistic creativity. *Psychoanalytic Quarterly, 45,* 185–212.

Penrose, R. (1989). *The emperor's new mind.* Oxford: Oxford University Press.

Peterson, N. (1989). *The relationship between affective expression in fantasy play and self-esteem in third grade children.* Unpublished masters' thesis, Case Western Reserve University, Cleveland, OH.

Piaget, J. (1967). *Play, dreams, and imitation in childhood.* New York: Norton. (Original work published 1945)

Pine, R., & Holt, R. (1960). Creativity and primary process: A study of adaptive regression. *Journal of Abnormal and Social Psychology, 61,* 370–379.

Prentky, R. (1989). Creativity and Psychopathology: Gamboling at the seat of madness. In J. Glover, R. Ronning, & C. R. Reynolds (Eds.), *Handbook of creativity* (pp. 243–271). New York: Plenum.

Rapaport, D. (1951). *Organization and pathology of thought.* New York: Columbia University Press.

Regis, E. (1987). *Who got Einstein's office?* Reading, PA: Addison-Wesley.

Reisman, J. (1973). *Principles of psychotherapy with children.* New York: Wiley.

Richards, R. (1990). Everyday creativity, eminent creativity, and health: Afterview for CRT issues on creativity and health. *Creativity Research Journal, 3,* 300–326.

Richards, R., & Kinney, P. (1990). Mood swings and creativity. *Creativity Research Journal, 3,* 202–217.

Rholes, W., Riskind J., & Lane, J. (1987). Emotional states and memory biases: Effects of cognitive priming and mood. *Journal of Personality and Social Psychology, 52,* 91–99.

Roe, A. (1951). A psychological study of physical scientists. *Genetic Psychology Monographs, 43,* 121–235.

Roe, A. (1952). A psychologist examines 64 eminent scientists. *Scientific American, 187,* 21–25.

Roe, A. (1953). *The making of a scientist.* New York: Dodd, Mead.

Roe, A. (1972). Patterns in the productivity of scientists. *Science, 176,* 940–941.

Rogers, C. (1954). Towards a theory of creativity. *E.T.C. A Review of General Semantics, 16,* 249–263.

Rogolsky, M. M. (1968). Artistic creativity and adaptive regression in third grade children. *Journal of Projective Techniques and Personality Assessment, 32,* 53–62.

Rohner, R. P. (1986). *The warmth dimension.* Beverly Hills, CA: Sage.

Rosenberg, N. (1987). *Creative drama and imagination.* Holt, Rhinehart & Winston.

Rosenthal, R., Baratz, S., & Hall, C. M. (1974). Teacher behavior, teacher expectations, and gains in pupils' rated creativity. *Journal of Genetic Psychology, 124,* 115–121.

Rothenberg, A. (1990). Creativity, mental health, and alcoholism. *Creativity Research Journal, 3,* 179–201.

Rothstein, M. (1991, June 19). The American who would be Beckett. *The New York Times.* pp. B, 1–2

Rubenstein, D. (1991, August). *Domain differences in creativity: A psychoeconomic perspective.* Paper presented at the meeting of the American Psychological Association, Washington, DC.

Rubin, K., Fein, G., Vandenberg. B. (1983). Play. In P. Mussen (Ed.). *Handbook of child psychology* (Vol. 4, pp. 693–774). New York: Wiley.

Runco, M. A. (1991). *Divergent thinking.* Norwood, NJ: Ablex.

Runco, M. A. (in press). Creative sequelae of tension and disequilibrium. In M. Shaw & M. A. Runco (Eds.), *Creativity and affect.* Norwood, NJ: Ablex.

Russ, S., (1980). Primary process integration on the Rorschach and achievement in children. *Journal of Personality Assessment, 44,* 338–344.

Russ, S. (1981). Primary process on the Rorschach and achievement in children: A follow-up study. *Journal of Personality Assessment, 46,* 473–477.

Russ, S. (1982). Sex differences in primary process thinking and flexibility in problem solving in children. *Journal of Personality Assessment, 45,* 569–577.

Russ, S. (1987). Assessment of cognitive affective interaction in children: Creativity, fantasy, and play research. In J. Butcher & C. Spielberger (Eds.), *Advances in personality assessment,* (Vol. 6, pp. 141–155). Hillsdale, NJ: Lawrence Erlbaum Associates.

Russ, S. (1988a). Primary process thinking in child development. In H. Lerner & P. Lerner (Eds.), *Primitive mental states and the Rorschach* (pp. 601–618). New York: International Universities Press.

Russ, S. (1988b). Primary process thinking on the Rorschach, divergent thinking, and coping in children. *Journal of Personality Assessment, 52,* 539–548.

Russ, S. & Grossman-McKee, A., (1990). Affective expression in children's fantasy play, primary process thinking on the Rorschach, and divergent thinking. *Journal of Personality Assessment, 54,* 756–771.

Russ, S., Grossman-Mckee, A., & Rutkin, Z. (1984). [Affect in Play Scale: Pilot Project]. Unpublished raw data.

Russ, S., & Peterson, N. (1990). *The Affect in Play Scale: Predicting creativity and coping in children.* Manuscript submitted for publication.

Saltz, E., Dixon, D., & Johnson, J. (1977). Training disadvantaged preschoolers on various fantasy activities: Effects on cognitive functioning and impulse control. *Child Development, 48,* 367–380.

Sarnoff, C. (1976) *Latency.* New York: Aronson.

Schachter, S., & Singer, J. (1962). Cognitive, social and physiological determinants of emotional state. *Psychological Review, 69,* 379–398.

Schulberg, D. (1990). Schizotypal and hypomanic traits, creativity, and psychological health. *Creativity Research Journal, 3,* 218–230.

Shaw, M. (1989). The eureka process: A structure for the creative experience in science and engineering. *Creativity Research Journal, 2,* 286–298.

Shaw, M. (in press). Affective components of scientific creativity. In M. Shaw & M. Runco (Eds.), *Creativity and affect.* Norwood, NJ: Ablex.

Sherrod, L., & Singer, J. (1979). The development of make-believe play. In J. Goldstein (Ed.), *Sports, games, and play* (pp. 1–28). Hillsdale, NJ: Lawrence Erlbaum Associates.

Simon, H. (1977). *Boston studies in the philosophy of science: Vol. 54: Models of discovery.* Boston: Reidel.

Simon, H. (1985, August). *Psychology of scientific discovery.* Paper presented at the annual meeting of the American Psychological Association, Los Angeles, CA.

Simon, H. (1988). Creativity and Motivation: A response to Csikszentmihalyi. *New Ideas in Psychology, 6,* 177–181.

Simonton, D. C. (1978). The eminent genius in history: The critical role of creative development. *Gifted Child Quarterly, 22,* 187–195.

Simonton, D. C. (1990a). History, chemistry, psychology, and genius: An intellectual autobiology of historiometry. In M. A. Runco & M. S. Albert (Eds.), *Theories of creativity* (pp. 92–115). Newbury Park, CA: Sage.

Simonton, D. C. (1990b). Political pathology and societal creativity. *Creativity Research Journal, 3,* 85–99.

Singer, D. L., & Rummo, J. (1973). Ideational creativity and behavioral style in kindergarten age children. *Developmental Psychology, 8,* 154–161.

Singer, D. L., & Singer, J. (1985). *Make believe: Games and activities to foster imaginative play in young children.* Glenview, IL: Scott, Foresman.

Singer, D. L., & Singer, J. (1990). *The House of Make-Believe.* Cambridge, MA: Harvard University Press.

Singer, J. L. (1973). *Child's world of make-believe.* New York: Academic Press.

Singer, J. L. (1981). *Daydreaming and fantasy.* New York: Oxford University Press.

Singer, J. L., & Singer, D. L. (1976). Imaginative play and pretending in early childhood: Some experimental approaches. In A. Davids (Ed.), *Child personality and psychopathology* (Vol. 3, pp. 69–112). New York: Wiley.

Singer, J. L., & Singer, D. L. (1981). *Television, imagination, and aggression.* Hillsdale, NJ: Lawrence Erlbaum Associates.

Sinnott, E. (1970). The creativeness of life. In P. C. Vernon (Ed.), *Creativity* (pp 107–115). Middlesex, England: Penguin Books.

Smilansky, S. (1986). *The effects of sociodiamatic play on disadvantaged preschool children.* New York: Wiley.

Smith, P. K., & Whitney, S. (1987). Play and associative fluency: Experimenter effects may be responsible for positive results. *Developmental Psychology, 23,* 49–53.

Smock, C., & Holt, R. (1962). Children's reactions to novelty: An experimental study of curiosity motivation. *Child Development, 33,* 631–642.

Smolucha, F. (1992). A reconstruction of Vygotsky's theory of creativity. *Creativity Research Journal, 5,* 49–67.

Snow, R. (1991, August). *Cognitive, affect, and individuality in Educational improvement.* Paper presented at the meeting of the American Psychological Association, San Francisco.

Spielberger, C. D. (1973). *State-trait anxiety inventory for children.* Palo Alto, CA: Consulting Psychological Press.

Spielberger, C. D., Peters, R., & Frain, F. (1981). Curiosity and anxiety. In H. G. Voss & H. Keller (Eds.), *Curiosity research: Basic concepts and results* [in German]. Weinheim, Federal Republic of Germany: Beltz.

Spielberger, C. D., & Starr, L. M. (in press). Curiosity and exploratory behavior. In H. F. O'Neil, Jr., & M. Drillings (Eds.), *Motivation: Research and Theory.* Hillsdale, NJ: Lawrence Erlbaum Associates.

Stallworthy, J. (1963). *Between the lines: Yeats poetry in the making.* Oxford: Clarendon Press.

Stein, M. T. (1971). Several findings of a transactional approach to creativity. In G. A. Steiner (Ed.), *The creative organization.* Chicago: University of Chicago Press.

Sternberg, R. (1988). A three-facet model of creativity. In R. Sternberg (Ed.), *The nature of creativity* (pp. 125–147), Cambridge: Cambridge University Press.

Sternberg, R., & Davidson, J. (1982, June). The mind of the puzzler. *Psychology Today, 16,* 37–44.

Sternberg, R. J., & Davidson, J. E. (1985). Cognitive development in the gifted and talented. In F. W. Horowitz & M. O'Brien (Eds.), *The gifted and talented.* Washington, DC: American Psychological Association.

Sternberg, R., & Lybart, T. (1991) An investment theory of creativity and its development. *Human Development, 34,* 1–31.

Suler, J. (1980). Primary process thinking and creativity. *Psychological Bulletin, 88,* 144–165.

Sutton-Smith, B. (1966). Piaget on play: A critique. *Psychological Review, 73,* 104–110.

Tegano, P., & Moran J. (1989) Sex differences in the original thinking of preschool and elementary school children. *Creativity Research Journal, 2,* 102–110.

Tellegen, A. (1989, August). Discussant. In L. Clark & D. Watson (Chair). *The emotional bases of personality.* Symposium conducted at the meeting of the American Psychological Association, New Orleans.

Thurstone, L. (1952). Creative talent. In L. Thurstone (Ed.), *Applications of psychology* (pp. 18–37). New York: Harper & Row.

Tomkins, S. S. (1962). *Affect, imagery, consciousness, Vol. 1: The positive affects.* New York: Springer.

Tomkins, S. S. (1963). *Affect, imagery, consciousness, Vol. 2: The negative affects.* New York: Springer.

Toplyn, G., & Maguire, W. (1991). The differential effect of noise on creative task performance. *Creativity Research Journal, 4,* 337–346.

Torrance, E. P. (1967, December). *Understanding the fourth grade slump in creativity.* (Final Report). Athens, GA: Georgia University.

Torrance, E. P. (1987). *The blazing drive: The creative personality.* Buffalo, NY: Bearly limited.

Torrance, E. P. (1988). The nature of creativity as manifest in its testing. In R. Sternberg (Ed.), *The nature of creativity* (pp. 43–75). Cambridge: Cambridge University Press.

Updike, J. (1989) *Self-consciousness.* New York: Knopf.

Urist J. (1980). The continuum between primary and secondary process thinking: Toward a concept of borderline thought. In J. Kwawer, H. Lerner, P. Lerner, & A. Sugarman(Eds.), *Borderline phenomena and the Rorschach test* (pp. 133–154). New York: International Universities Press.

Vernon, P. E. (1970). *Creativity.* Harmondsworth, UK: Methuin.

Vernon, P. E. (1989). The nature–nurture problem in creativity. In J. Glover, R. Ronning, & C. R. Reynolds (Eds.), *Handbook of creativity* (pp. 93–110). New York: Plenum.

Vinacke, W. E. (1952). *Psychology of thinking.* New York: McGraw-Hill.

Voss, J. & Means, M. (1989). Toward a model of creativity based upon problem solving in the social sciences. In J. Glover, R. Ronning, & C. R. Reynolds (Eds.). *Handbook of creativity* (pp. 399–410). New York: Plenum.

Vygotsky, L. S. (1967). Vaobraszeniye i tvorchestvo v deskom voraste [Imagination and creativity in childhood]. Moscow: Prosvescheniye. (Original work published 1930)

Waelder, R. (1933). Psychoanalytic theory of play. *Psychoanalytic Quarterly, 2,* 208–224.

Walberg, H. (1988). Creativity and talent as learning. In R. Sternberg (Ed.), *The Nature of creativity.* Cambridge: Cambridge University Press.

Wallach, M. (1970). Creativity. I. P. Mussen (Ed.), *Carmichael's manual of child psychology* (Vol. 1, pp. 1211–1272). New York: Wiley.

Wallach, M., & Kogan, N. (1965). *Modes of thinking in young children: A study of the creativity–intelligence distinction.* New York: Holt, Rinehart & Winston.

Wallas, C. (1926). *The art of thought.* New York: Harcourt Brace.

Weisberg, R. (1986). *Creativity: Genius and other myths.* New York: Freiman.

Weisberg, R. (1988) Problem solving and creativity. In R. Sternberg (Ed.), *The nature of creativity* (pp. 148–176). Cambridge: Cambridge University Press.

Winnecott, D. W. (1971). *Playing & reality.* New York: Tavistock.

Zajonc, R. (1980). Feeling and thinking: Preferences need no inferences. *American Psychologist, 35,* 151–175.

Zajonc, R. (1991, August). *Emotions and brain temperature.* Paper presented at the meeting of the American Psychological Association, Boston.

Zeitlin, S. (1980). Assessing coping behavior. *American Journal of Orthopsychiatry, 50,* 139–144.

Zimiles, H. (1981). Cognitive-affective interaction: A concept that exceeds the researcher's grasp. In E. Shapiro & E. Weber (Eds.). *Cognitive and affective growth* (pp. 49–63). Hillsdale, NJ: Lawrence Erlbaum Associates.

Author Index

A

Adaman, J., 74
Adler, T., 92
Albert, R. S., 64, 92
Alessandri, S., 96
Allison, O., 24
Alvin, R., 19
Amabile, T., 7, 15, 58, 75, 76, 86, 92, 93, 96, 97, 103, 107
Ames, L., 26
Anastasi, A., 15, 69
Andreasen, N. J. C., 65
Arieti, S., 18, 20
Arlin, P. K., 4
Arlow, J., 20
Armbruster, B., 3
Axline, V., 39, 89

B

Bachelor, P., 107
Bandura, A., 29
Baratz, S., 93
Barden, R., 37, 39, 40, 74
Barron, F., 11, 60, 62, 63, 75, 104
Beard, D., 22
Begley, S., 84
Berlyne, D. E., 77
Blatt, S., 24
Block, J. W., 90, 91

Block, J., 90, 91
Bower, G. H., 19, 73, 80
Brenner, C., 20
Bush, M., 20
Butcher, H. J., 60

C

Canter, A., 65
Canter, S., 66
Cattell, R. B., 51, 60, 65
Claridge, G., 66
Clark, D., 81
Clark, M., 73
Clement, J., 67
Cohen, I., 24
Corliss, R., 21
Costa, P. T., 11, 14, 61, 62, 83, 105
Cropley, A., 64, 97
Crutchfield, R., 76
Csikszentmihalyi, M., 4, 7, 11, 62, 69, 76, 85, 86, 91, 94, 96, 97, 108
Culbane, J., 21
Currie, J., 94

D

Dansky, J., 32, 34, 35, 36
Daubman, K., 7, 14, 40, 58, 71, 72, 81, 83, 103

Davidson, J. E., 6
Davidson, J., 108
Davis, S., 3
Dixon, D., 33, 41
Dorfman, E., 89
Drevdahl, J. E., 65
Dudek, S., 14, 17, 23, 25, 28, 69, 93, 107
Duncker, K., 72

E

Easterbrook, J. A., 74
Ebbesen, E., 39, 71
Erikson, E. N., 41
Evans, T. D., 93
Exner, J., 30

F

Fein, G. C., 32, 38, 43
Feirstein, A., 24
Feist, G., 67
Feldman, D. H., 108
Felleman, E., 37, 39
Festinger, L., 63
Fischer, K., 18
Ford, M., 39, 40, 74
Frain, F., 77
Franklin, M., 108
Freedheim, D., 39, 42, 89
Freud, A., 39, 89
Freud, S., 17, 19, 20

G

Gamble, K., 25
Gardner, H., 94, 108
Gardner, R., 7
Gedo, J., 98
Gerard, D., 92
Getzels, J. W., 93
Getzels, S., 4, 11, 62
Ghiselin, B., 22
Ginott, H., 89
Giovacchini, P., 20
Golann, S. E., 1
Gough, H., 11, 63, 64
Greene, T., 75
Grossman-McKee, A., 14, 28, 30, 31, 37, 42, 46, 47, 52, 54, 58
Gruber, H. E., 3, 4
Gryskiewicz, N., 96
Guilford, J. P., 4, 5, 11, 27, 33

H

Hall, C. M., 93
Hanlas, M., 81
Harrington, D., 11, 60, 90, 91, 104
Harter, S., 53
Hasenfus, N., 82
Havel, J., 23
Hayes, J., 1
Heinicke, C., 26
Heinzen, T., 63
Helson, R., 63, 64, 98
Hines, D., 82
Hocevar, D., 107
Holt, R. R., 17, 18, 19
Holt, R., 14, 23, 24, 25, 26, 28, 30, 45, 75
Howe, P., 38, 43
Hudspith, S., 82
Hughes, R., 98
Hume, W. I., 66
Hunt, J., 92

I

Isen, A., 7, 14, 40, 58, 71, 72, 73, 81, 82, 103
Izard, C. E., 7, 45, 76

J

Jacklin, C., 29
Jackson, P., 93
James, W., 77
Jamison, K., 65
Jaspers, J., 51
Jausovec, N., 15, 71, 72, 81
Johnson, G., 85
Johnson, J., 33, 41
Jones, R., 6, 85
Julisch, B., 73

K

Kagan, J., 29
Karp, L., 73
Kellner, H., 25
Kinney, P., 65
Klein, G., 7
Kleinman, M., 29
Klinger, E., 33
Kogan, N., 5, 7, 28, 29, 30, 32, 33, 34, 35, 36, 37
Krause, W., 73

Kris, E., 4, 20, 24, 66, 82, 83
Krystal, A., 85
Krystal, H., 85
Kuhn, T., 67

L

Lane, J., 19, 73, 80, 81
Lange-Eichbaum, W., 65
Langley, P., 6, 85
Lazarus, R., 18, 81
Leavitt, E., 27
LeDoux, J. E., 81
Lieberman, J. N., 14, 36, 38, 40, 49
Luchins, A., 27
Luchins, E., 27
Lybart, T., 70

M

Maccoby, E., 29
MacKinnon, D. W., 1, 11, 60, 65, 75, 86,
    92
Maddi, S., 33
Maguire, W., 74
Magyari-Beck, L., 108
Martindale, C., 19, 20, 22, 60, 63, 66, 82,
    104
Masters, J., 37, 39, 40, 74
McCrae, R. R., 11, 14, 61, 62, 83, 105
McNeil, T. F., 65
Means, M., 14, 62, 103
Mednick, S., 80
Mendelsohn, G. A., 82
Metcalfe, J., 6, 15
Michael, W., 107
Michel, M., 93
Middlebrook, D. W., 66, 99
Milgram, R., 37, 58
Miller, B. C., 92
Milos, M., 38
Mischel, W., 39, 71
Mitchell, A. R., 65
Moore, B., 7
Moran, J., 29
Morgan, F. T., 29
Moriarity, A., 7
Moss, H. A., 29
Moustakas, C., 39
Murray, J., 25, 28

N

Natale, M., 81
Niederland, W., 67
Noice, H., 75
Nowicki, G., 7, 14, 40, 58, 71, 72, 81, 83,
    103

P

Paraskevopoulos, J., 92
Penrose, R., 84
Peters, R., 77
Peterson, N., 37, 50, 52, 53, 58
Piaget, J., 33
Pine, R., 14, 19, 24, 25, 28, 75
Pipp, S., 18
Prentky, R., 65, 66

R

Rapaport, D., 19
Regis, E., 97
Reisman, J., 89
Reiss, S., 38
Rholes, W., 19, 73, 80, 81
Richards, R., 65, 83
Riskind, J., 19, 73, 80, 81
Roe, A., 11, 60, 65, 69
Rogers, C., 90, 98
Rogolsky, M. M., 26
Rohner, R. P., 94
Rosenberg, N., 94
Rosenthal, R., 93
Rothenberg, A., 68
Rothstein, M., 68
Rubenstein, D., 98
Rubin, K., 38, 43
Rummo, J., 36, 40, 49
Runco, M. A., 5, 7, 11, 14, 37, 63, 92, 103
Russ, S. W., 7, 14, 19, 23, 25, 26, 27, 28,
    29, 30, 31, 37, 39, 42, 43, 46, 47, 50, 52,
    53, 58, 72, 81, 83, 89
Rutkin, Z., 46

S

Saltz, E., 33, 41
Sarnoff, C., 41
Schachter, S., 39
Schaefer, C., 15, 69

Schulberg, D., 65
Shalker, T. E., 73
Shaw, M., 7, 63, 69
Sherrod, L., 33
Silverman, F., 34
Silvern, L., 38, 43
Simon, H., 6, 85, 87
Simonton, D. C., 97, 98
Singer, D. L., 33, 36, 38, 40, 41, 49, 74, 90, 92, 94, 106
Singer, J. L., 32, 33, 36, 38, 39, 40, 41, 45, 49, 74, 90, 92, 94, 106
Sinnott, E., 3
Smilansky, S., 94, 96
Smith, P. K., 34, 35, 36, 52, 107
Smock, C., 26
Smolucha, F., 33
Snow, R., 94
Spielberger, C. D., 54, 77
Stallworthy, J., 22
Starr, L. M., 77
Stein, M. T., 65
Sternberg, R., 6, 11, 62, 63, 70, 73, 108
Suler, J., 18, 20, 24, 25, 28, 67
Sutton-Smith, B., 34

T

Teasdale, J., 81
Tegano, P., 29
Tellegen, A., 7
Thurstone, L., 2
Tomkins, S. S., 38, 45
Toplyn, G., 74
Torrance, E. P., 2, 4, 69, 93

U

Updike, J., 69
Urist, J., 18

V

Vandenberg, B., 38, 43
Vernon, P. E., 2, 22, 62
Verreault, R., 14, 25, 28
Vinacke, W. E., 4
Voss, J., 14, 62, 103
Vygotsky, L. S., 33

W

Waelder, R., 40, 42
Walberg, H., 95
Walker, R., 26
Wallach, M., 5, 28, 29, 33, 102
Wallas, C., 3, 4
Weisberg, R., 3, 6, 11
Whitney, S., 34, 35, 36, 52, 107
Winnecott, D. W., 41
Woolf, V. C., 68
Wright, C., 107

Z

Zajonc, R., 19, 81
Zeiss, A., 39, 71
Zeitlin, S., 53
Zimiles, H., 8, 19

Subject Index

A

Adjustment and creativity, 64–67
Affect in Play Scale, 43–59, 110–118
  future research, 58–59, 102, 104
  play task, 43–44, 110–111
  rating scale, 44–46, 111–118
  reliability, 47, 52, 54, 58
  stability of scores, 54–55
  validity, 46–54
Affect states, *see also* mood-induction,
  12–14, 32, 39–40, 102–103
Affect-laden thoughts, *see also* primary
  process thinking, 12–14, 32, 39–41,
  101–102
Affective processes, 7–8, 12–13, 39–42,
  101–105
  emotion and affect, 7
  future research, 106
  measures of, 8, 30–31, 43–59
  model of affect and creativity, 8–16, 39,
  100–105
Artificial intelligence, 6–7, 84–87
  and affect, 85–87
Artistic creativity, 1–2, 65, 67–70, 83, 102

B

Breadth of knowledge, 11, 63, 101

C

Challenge, preference for, 12–14, 62–63,
  103–105
Cognitive creative processes, *see also*
  divergent thinking and *see also*
  transformation abilities, 4–7, 8–11,
  101
  Guilford's processes, 4–6, 9–11
Cognitive style, 7, 19, 26
Complexity, preference for, 12, 14, 62–63,
  104–105
Computer simulation, *see* Artificial
  intelligence
Critical thinking, *see* evaluative ability
Curiosity, 12, 77–78, 104–105

D

Definitions of creativity, 2, *see also*
  Products, creative
Descriptions of creativity, 21–23
  Poncaire, 22
  Robin Williams, 21
Divergent thinking, 5, 9, 21, 27–30,
  30–34, 37, 45–52, 67, 101–103,
  107

E

Enhancing creativity, 88–99
  in childrearing, 90–93
  in play, 89–90
  psychotherapy, 98–99
  in school, 93–96
    use of play, 94–96
  societal factors, 97–98
  in work environments, 96–98
  in universities, 97
Evaluative ability, 11, 15, 22, 101

F

Fantasy, 32–34, 46
Flow, 86, 96
Free association, 9, 21, 40, 66, 80

G

Gender differences, 26–30, 47–50, 63–64,
  68, 74–75, 98, 102, 106

I

Incubation stage, 3, 15, 16
Insight abilities, 6, 11, 15, 73, 101–103
Intelligence and creativity, 4–5
Intrinsic motivation, 12, 15, 75–76, 104–105

H

Holt Scoring System for the Rorschach,
  23–31

L

Luchins' Water-Jar Test, 27, 72

M

Model of affect and creativity, 8–16, 39,
  100–105
Mood and memory work, 80–81
  Bower's associative network 19, 73–74,
    80, 82–84, 101
Mood-induction, 14, 39–40, 58–59, 71–75,
  103
Motivational systems, *see* curiosity and *see*
  intrinsic motivation

N

Neurological theories of creativity, 79–84

O

Openness to experience, 12, 14, 61–62,
  104–105

P

Passion and creativity, 69–70, 103–104
Personality traits and creativity, 11–16,
  60–64
  and affect, 104–105
Play, *see also* primary process and play
  affective expression in, 37–42, 75
  and cognitive processes, 32–34
  and coping, 50–54
  enhancing creativity in play (see
    enhancing creativity)
  measures of, 38, 43–59
  methodological issues in play research,
    34–37
  research directions, 106–107
Playfulness, 40
Primary process thinking, 12, 17–31
  and affect, 18–20
  definition, 17–18
  and neurological processes, 74, 82–84
  in play, 40–41, 45, 47–50, 84
  on Rorschach, 23–31
Problem finding, 4, 11, 101
Product, creative, 1–3
  criteria for, 1–2, 5–8
  measures of, 107–108
Psychosis and creativity, *see* adjustment

R

Regression in the service of the ego, 4,
  20–21, 42, 66, 83
Repression, 18, 20, 73
Risk-taking, 12, 15, 63, 104

S

Scientific creativity, 65, 67–70
Self-confidence, 12, 14, 15, 60, 63,
  104–105

Sexton, Anne, 66, 99
Stages, 3–4
    Wallas' stages, 3, 5, 15–16

T

Tolerance of ambiguity, 12, 14, 62, 104–105
Transformation abilities, 5, 10, 13–14, 21,
    27, 72, 101–103

U

Unconscious processes, 22
Updike, John, 69–70

W

Woolf, Virginia, 68